Partridge Genealogy

PARTRIDGE MANOR HOUSE, WISHANGER, GLOUCESTERSHIRE, ENGLAND.

PARTRIDGE GENEALOGY.

DESCENDANTS OF JOHN PARTRIDGE

OF

MEDFIELD, MASS.

BY

GEORGE HOMER PARTRIDGE, B.S.

BOSTON:
PRESS OF DAVID CLAPP & SON.
1904.

eprinted in Part from New-England Historical and Genealogical Register.

INTRODUCTION.

IN the following pages will be found brief records of nearly all male descendants of John Partridge, of Medfield, Mass., for six generations. The author regrets that lack of time prevented him from arranging for publication in this volume the mass of material regarding later generations which he has collected in a correspondence extending over several years. To those who have been kind enough to answer his inquiries and to all interested in the subject he desires to announce his intention of compiling a comprehensive genealogy of all branches of the Partridge family in America; and to this end he seeks the co-operation of all who bear the name or who are bound by ties of blood.

It may be well to state here that there were four principal and distinct families of this name who came to New England between the years 1630 and 1650. These the author designates as the Medfield, Duxbury, Hadley and Salisbury branches, from the towns where their founders settled and died. So far as can be learned none of these bears any relationship to any other; but it is not improbable that they could be traced to a single source in the centuries following the English conquest.

In the year 1066, at the historic battle of Hastings, William, duke of Normandy, defeated Harold, then king of England, and ascended the English throne; and to his new possessions he soon added his own little duchy of Normandy. To those of his fellow-countrymen who had assisted him in his work of conquest William made grants of land in the conquered kingdom, the number and size of which depended upon the value of the service rendered; and this policy was continued by William's successors in the wars of the next century. To accomplish this the estates of the British nobles were seized and confiscated, and the bold and intrepid men of Normandy became the landed gentry of England.

Among those who thus received grants from the Crown was one described by English antiquarians as "Partridge the Norman." He is said to have migrated during the reign of Stephen (1135–1154) and, in recognition of his military services, to have received from Henry II. (1154–1189) estates in Essex, though the family afterwards settled in Gloucestershire. Certain it is that, in the next century (1254), Richard de Pertriche (that being the Norman and

original spelling of the name) is indisputably recorded as the head
of the family, with manors in the county of Gloucester. These
royal grants not only prove the family to have been in favor at
Court, but at once mark it as one of ancient distinction.

Of these manors, or family seats, the one at Wishanger, though
not the oldest, is perhaps the most interesting. "The Hamlet of
Wishanger," writes Rev. Francis Partridge, D.D., of Frederickton,
New Brunswick," is situated about one mile north-west of Miserden.
Osculf Musard, of Musarden (as it was formerly spelled), gave
Wishanger (then called Riscanger, now pronounced Wessinger) as
a foundation for an establishment of Knights Templars, from whom
it passed to the Knights of St. John of Jerusalem, who held it till
their dissolution. It was afterwards granted to Sir Thomas Palmer
in the sixth year of the reign of Edward VI. (1553). He was
attainted of high treason in trying to seat Lady Jane Grey upon
the throne, and executed, and his estates confiscated. In the first
year of the reign of Queen Mary (1553) the estate of Wishanger
was granted to William Lord Howard. Christopher Bumstead, for
some reason, levied a fine upon the manor, and in the fourth year
of Mary (1557) this estate came, for the first time, into the hands
of the Partridge family."

The manor house itself is very quaint and picturesque, as may be
seen from the cut herewith presented. It was rebuilt and a porch
added in 1578 by Robert Partridge, then head of the house, and the
impaled coat of arms of Robert and his wife Anne may still be
seen, carved in stone over the front entrance. [See Burke's "Landed
Gentry," vol. ii., pp. 1056-57.] John Partridge, of Wishanger,
seems to be the one to whom this estate was originally granted.
He was succeeded by his son William, who was member of parlia-
ment for Rochester in the fourteenth year of Elizabeth (1572).
Miles Partridge, brother of William, was a man of note, and one
who played a prominent part in the history of those troublesome
times. He was High Sheriff of Gloucestershire during the last years
of the reign of Henry VIII. (1509-1547), and received from that
monarch a grant of the manor of Almondsbury (Amesbury). He
was a friend and comrade of the unfortunate Duke of Somerset,
whom he accompanied in his Scottish expedition, and was knighted
for conspicuous bravery on the battlefield of Pinkie (September 10,
1547). After Somerset's fall Sir Miles Partridge appears to have
been gallantly protecting the person of the Duchess, and was ar-
rested in her house and executed, February 26, 1552. An account
of the trial and execution of the Duke of Somerset and his so-called
confederates, Vane, Partridge, Stanhope and Arundel, may be
found in Froude's "History of England," volume v., chapter 28.
It is interesting to note that, when the charge of treason could not
be proven, "felony" was the indictment on which, at the instigation
of the hated Duke of Northumberland, these men were put to death.

While it is to be regretted that, of the four American families of this name, only the Salisbury branch can be traced to this distinguished house in Gloucestershire, yet it may serve as an incentive to some who may have the wish and means to pursue a systematic research in England to state that very little has yet been attempted in the way of investigation. The field would, without doubt, prove fruitful, and with the knowledge of an ancient and historic lineage it is to be hoped that some one may undertake the task.

The author has received so generous and universal a response to his letters of inquiry that he feels that an expression of appreciation to each and all of his correspondents will not be out of place. To Mr. William H. Partridge, of Boston, Mass., who has done more than any other to stimulate an interest in the history of our family, he is especially grateful. Awaiting the early publication of a complete Partridge genealogy, this volume is herewith closed.

THE AUTHOR.

NEW YORK, January 1, 1904.

THE PARTRIDGE GENEALOGY.

DESCENDANTS OF JOHN PARTRIDGE, OF MEDFIELD, MASS.

1. JOHN[1] PARTRIDGE came to Medfield from Dedham in 1653, and was probably accompanied by his brother William and sister Margery. He was in Dedham at least a year earlier than that, for on "ye 7 of ye 1 Mo. 1652" he shared with others in the division of 500 acres of land. (Dedham Town Records, vol. iii., p. 211.) Prior to these dates, nothing concerning them can yet be stated with certainty. It may be well, however, for the benefit of those who may desire to extend their researches to England, to call attention to the fact that in the Visitation of Essex (Harl. Soc. Pub., xiii., part 1, p. 465), which was made in the year 1634, the children of Captain John Partridge, of Navestock, were John, aged about fourteen years, William, Jane and Margerett. From information obtained from the vicar of the parish of Navestock, in 1899, by Mr. Frank Harvey Partridge, of New York, it appears that, of the foregoing children, William was born in 1622, and Margerett in 1628. In his will, made Aug. 14, 1692, William Partridge, of Medfield, states his age as " about seventy years" (Suffolk Co. Prob. Rec., vol. xiii., p. 75). In the will of Margery Stacy, of Medfield, relict widow of Thomas Mason, made in 1695, the testatrix states her age as "about sixty and seven years" (Suffolk Co. Prob. Rec., vol. xx., p. 281). These coincidences, while they prove nothing, should, it seems to the writer, be given consideration in clearing up the mystery of the English origin of the Medfield Partridges.

John and William Partridge took up their house lots in Medfield in "The bachelors Roe," now North street (Medfield Records). Their places were near together, and one of their neighbors in the same street was Thomas Mason, whom Margery Partridge married, April 23, 1653. This is the first marriage recorded in Medfield (Tilden's Hist. of Medfield, p. 429). John and William both signed the proprietors' agreement drawn, it is supposed, by Ralph Wheelock, the founder of Medfield (Tilden's Hist. of Medfield, p. 38). They appear to have been useful citizens, each serving the town as selectman, and John being chosen clerk of the market in 1672. In 1676, at the burning of Medfield by the Indians, John's house and barn were destroyed, together with a quantity of grain and several head of cattle (Tilden's Hist. of Medfield, p. 95). William married twice. He had a numerous family, and his descendants will be treated of in a subsequent paper. This article, which the compiler hopes at some time to extend, will be confined to five generations of the descendants of John Partridge.

John Partridge married, Dec. 18, 1655, Magdalen, daughter of John and Magdalen Bullard, early of Watertown and later of Medfield. She died in Medfield, Dec. 27, 1677. He died May 28, 1706, and in his will, proved June 25 following (Suffolk Co. Prob. Rec., vol. xvi., pp. 158–159), mention is made of his sons John, Eleazer, Samuel and Zachariah; his daughter Rachel, wife of Theophilus Clark; and three of his grandchildren, Eleazer and Obadiah Adams, and Hannah Rockwood.

Children:

2. i. JOHN,[2] b. Sept. 21, 1656; d. Dec. 9, 1743.
   ii. HANNAH, b. April 15, 1658; d. March 8, 1680; m. April 2, 1679, Joseph, b. Medfield, 1659, d. Swansea, July 21, 1693, son of Nicholas and Margaret (Holbrook) Rockwood. They resided in Medfield, he afterwards in Swansea. One child.
   iii. DEBORAH, b. Aug. 16, 1662; m. Apr. 4, 1681, John, b. Medfield, Feb. 18, 1657, d. Medway, Mch. 1, 1751, son of Edward and Lydia (Rockwood) Adams. They resided in Medfield (now Millis). Children.
3. iv. ELEAZER, b. Feb. 20, 1664; d. Nov. 8, 1736.
   v. ABIEL, b. June 13, 1667; d. July 2, 1667.
   vi. EXPERIENCE, b. June 13, 1667; d. July 5, 1667.
   vii. RACHEL, b. July 12, 1669; d. Dec. 1, 1717; m. Theophilus, b. Medfield, Sept. 25, 1670, d. Oct. 7, 1737, son of Benjamin and Dorcas (Morse) Clark. They resided in Medfield (now Rockville). Several children.
4. viii. SAMUEL, b. Feb. 22, 1671; d. Dec. 12, 1752.
5. ix. ZACHARIAH, b. July 2, 1674; d. Sept. 23, 1716.
   x. MARY, d. Feb. 15, 1677.

2. JOHN[2] PARTRIDGE (*John*[1]) was born in Medfield, Sept. 21, 1656. He settled in what is now Millis, in 1681. He was one of the first to take up his residence in that portion of Medfield lying west of Charles river, and was active in having it set off as the town of Medway, in 1713 (Tilden's Hist. of Medfield, p. 451). In 1710, he was chosen master of a school established for residents of the west side. He was interested in church matters, and was a deacon of the Medway church (Jameson's Hist. of Medway, p. 121). He was present at Deerfield when news was received of the return of the captives taken at the Deerfield massacre, and is said to have himself made a copy of Benjamin Waite's letter announcing their arrival at Albany, which, in company with John Plimpton, Jr., he brought to Medfield and delivered to the Rev. John Wilson, by whom it was forwarded to the Governor of the Colony (Sheldon's Hist. of Deerfield, vol. i., p. 186; Tilden's Hist. of Medfield, p. 458).

He married three times: first, Dec. 24, 1678, Elizabeth, born in Medfield, April 3, 1657, died July 22, 1688, daughter of Nicholas and Margaret (Holbrook) Rockwood; second, Elizabeth, born in Medfield, March 18, 1666, died Aug. 14, 1719, daughter of Jonathan and Elizabeth (Fussell) Adams; third, April 17, 1721, Hannah, born in Sherborn, April 18, 1663, died July 19, 1754, daughter of William and Mary Sheffield. He died in Medway, Dec. 9, 1743. His will was proved Sept. 4, 1744 (Suffolk Co. Prob. Rec., vol. xxxvii., p. 121). All his children are named. His youngest son, Stephen, received the homestead, but dying before his father, and the latter not making a new will, the property passed into the hands of Stephen's widow, who afterwards married Abner Ellis.

Children by first wife:

i. ELIZABETH,[3] b. Sept. 13, 1679; d. Apr. 25, 1706; m. Dec. 22, 1701, Ebenezer, b. Medfield, April 24, 1677, d. Medway, Jan. 29, 1767, son of Joseph and Mary (Fairbanks) Daniel. They resided in Medway. Children.
ii. MARY, b. Feb. 26, 1681; d. Feb. 14, 1754; m. Nov. 25, 1706, Ebenezer, son (says Blake's Hist. of Franklin) of John and Sarah Law-

rence, of Wrentham. He d. June 12, 1751. They resided in Wrentham. Children.

6. iii. JOHN, b. about 1683; d. Sept. 6, 1756.
7. iv. BENONI, b. May 25, 1687; d. Dec. 26, 1769.

Children by second wife:

8. v. JONATHAN, b. Nov. 25, 1693.
vi. HANNAH, b. Mch. 16, 1696; d. Oct. 12, 1751; m. May 7, 1713, Jeremiah, b. Medfield, Nov. 3, 1684, d. Medway, Nov. 16, 1771, son of Joseph and Mary (Fairbanks) Daniel. They resided in Medway. One child.
vii. DEBORAH, b. Mch. 1, 1698; d. Aug. 30, 1740; m. Israel, b. Bridge-water, Feb. 21, 1703, son of James and Mary Keith. They resided in Mendon and Uxbridge. Children.
9. viii. JAMES, b. Oct. 8, 1700; d. Mch. 9, 1769.
ix. SARAH, b. Jan. 8, 1702; m. Mch. 13, 1723, George, b. Medfield, Jan. 16, 1699, son of Peter and Experience (Cook) Adams. They re-sided in Medway until about 1735, afterwards in Wrentham. Chil-dren.
10. x. STEPHEN, b. April 16, 1706; d. Mch. 10, 1742.

3. ELEAZER[2] PARTRIDGE (*John*[1]) was born in Medfield, Feb. 20, 1664. He inherited his father's homestead in Medfield, and resided there until about 1723, when he purchased a tract of land in Bellingham, and removed there. This property was in the vicinity of what is now North Bellingham, which for a century and a half was known as Partridgetown, and is still so designated by the oldest inhabitants. He married twice: first, April 25, 1692, Elizabeth, born in Medfield, Feb. 29, 1671, died July 4, 1704, daughter of Samuel and Eliza-beth (Turner) Smith; second, Apr. 9, 1705, Elizabeth, daughter of William and Elizabeth (Twitchell) Allen, of Medfield. She died Oct. 26, 1733; and he died Nov. 8, 1736. His will was proved Dec. 2, 1736 (Suffolk Co. Prob. Rec., vol. xxxiii., p. 5). Bequests were made to his sons Eleazer, Job, Joseph, Benjamin and Zacha-riah; his daughter Abigail Clark; and three of his grandchildren, Joseph Ellis, Sarah Ellis and Reuben Ellis. His children were born in Medfield.

Children by first wife:

11. i. ELEAZER,[3] b. March 7, 1693.
ii. JOSEPH, b. May 16, 1695; d. in infancy.
iii. ELIZABETH, b. Aug. 16, 1696; d. Jan. 14, 1718; m. Dec. 12, 1716, Joseph, b. Medfield, Nov. 23, 1691, d. Medway, March 13, 1757, son of Joseph and Lydia (Lovell) Ellis. They resided in Medway. One son.
12. iv. JOB, b. May 19, 1698; d. Feb. 7, 1742.
v. ABIGAIL, b. March 23, 1700; d. April 17, 1750; m. Jan. 24, 1727, Ephraim, b. Medfield, Sept. 27, 1703, son of Samuel and Sarah (Pratt) Clark. They resided in Walpole. Children.
vi. RACHEL, b. March 11, 1702; d. Nov. 18, 1727; m. Nov. 26, 1723, David, b. Medfield, June 24, 1702, d. Bellingham, 1739, son of Eleazer and Mary (Metcalf) Ellis. They resided in Medfield, he after 1732 in Bellingham. Two children.
vii. SILENCE, b. June 19, 1704; d. Oct. 31, 1704.

Children by second wife:

13. viii. JOSEPH, b. March 15, 1706; d. June 22, 1772.
ix. DAVID, b. March 22, 1708; d. young.
x. PHEBE, b. Sept. 5, 1709; d. Nov. 12, 1709.
14. xi. BENJAMIN, b. May 16, 1713; d. Feb. 10, 1805.
xii. PETER, b. May 22, 1716; d. young.
15. xiii. ZACHARIAH, b. March 22, 1720; d. Feb. 7, 1799.

4. **SAMUEL² PARTRIDGE** (*John¹*) was born in Medfield, Feb. 22, 1671. He drew land in the Black Swamp in 1702 (Jameson's Hist. of Medway, p. 40). His lot lay along the Charles river in the south part of this tract, which, in 1713, became the town of Medway and is now Rockville. He took an active interest in this enterprise and was elected a member of the first board of selectmen. He was also a deacon of the Medway church (Jameson's Hist. of Medway, p. 121). He married, June 5, 1701, Hannah, born in Medfield, Sept. 3, 1676, daughter of Robert and Abigail (Eaton) Mason. She died in Medway, Aug. 21, 1750; and he died there, Dec. 12, 1752. In his will, made Jan. 23, 1745, probated Jan. 5, 1753 (Suffolk Co. Prob. Rec., vol. xlvii., p. 200), he mentions his daughters Hannah Fisher, Mehetabel Grant, Silence Kingsbury and Thankful Partridge; and his sons Samuel, Ebenezer, Joshua and Caleb. The latter was made executor.

Children:

i. HANNAH,³ b. April 6, 1702; m. (1) Feb. 2, 1725, Cornelius, b. Wrentham, Sept. 29, 1692, d. April 21, 1754, son of Cornelius and Anna (Whitney) Fisher. They resided in Wrentham. Children. (See Fisher Gen.) She m. (2) Daniel Hawes of Wrentham, and was living Feb., 1760.

ii. THANKFUL, b. Aug. 7, 1703.

16. iii. SAMUEL, b. Nov. 6, 1704; d. 1774.

17. iv. EBENEZER, b. May 29, 1706; d. May 15, 1794.

v. ABIGAIL, b. Nov. 7, 1707; d. Sept. 16, 1734.

vi. BENJAMIN, b. March 13, 1709; d. March 13, 1709.

vii. SILENCE, b. March 13, 1709; d. March 17, 1709.

viii. MEHETABEL, b. July 6, 1710; m. April 15, 1741, Joseph, b. Wrentham, Jan. 6, 1700, son of Benjamin and Priscilla Grant. She was his second wife. They resided in Wrentham. One or more children.

18. ix. JOSHUA, b. July 27, 1713; d. Jan. 19, 1795.

x. CALEB, b. March 17, 1717; d. Feb. 20, 1755. He m. Phebe ———, who received one-third of his estate. No children. She m. (2) July 7, 1755, Joseph Ankers of Boston.

xi. SILENCE, b. March 5, 1719; m. Dec. 23, 1742, Stephen, b. Wrentham, July 7, 1717, d. April 23, 1754, son of Daniel and Elizabeth (Stevens) Kingsbury. They resided in Wrentham. Children. (See Kingsbury Gen., incomplete regarding this family.)

5. **ZACHARIAH² PARTRIDGE** (*John¹*) was born in Medfield, July 2, 1674. He settled near his brother Samuel in the Black Swamp (Medway), where land was assigned him in 1702 (Jameson's Hist. of Medway, p. 41). He married, June 5, 1701, Mary, born in Medfield, March 7, 1686, died in Medway, Sept. 12, 1747, daughter of John and Mary (Herring) Ellis. Zachariah Partridge died Sept. 23, 1716, leaving no will. His widow married second, John Barber. On March 20, 1732, Edward Clark, John Adams and Timothy Clark, of Medway, were appointed "to appraise the lands and property of Zachariah Partridge, deceased, in order to settle the same upon his son Asa," who had just attained his majority (Suffolk Co. Deeds, vol. xxxi., p. 372). Payments were to be made to his sisters "Mary White, deceased, or her heirs," Magdalen Daniels, Sarah Partridge and Phebe Partridge; and his mother was to retain her right of dower for life. On Aug. 19, 1734, Asa Partridge died, unmarried, and the property was later distributed among the remaining heirs.

Children :

i. MARY,[3] b. April 11, 1702; m. Jan. 25, 1726, Benjamin White. They
  settled in Dudley, Mass.
ii. MAGDALEN, b. Feb. 4, 1704; d. Oct. 13, 1780; m. Feb. 11, 1724, David,
  b. Medfield, Feb. 21, 1699, son of Joseph Daniels. He d. Franklin,
  Nov. 19, 1781. They resided in Franklin. Children.
iii. SARAH, b. Oct. 9, 1706; m. Joseph Green.
iv. ZACHARIAH, b. April 7, 1709; d. Aug. 21, 1718.
v. ASA, b. March 11, 1711; d. Aug. 19, 1734.
vi. PHEBE, b. Aug. 27, 1714; m. William Smead, and removed to Upper
  Ashuelot (now Keene, N. H.).

6. JOHN[3] PARTRIDGE (*John*,[2] *John*[1]) was born in Medfield (now Millis),
   but the date of his birth is not recorded. He married, Feb. 3,
   1709, Anna, born in Wrentham, Oct. 2, 1689, daughter of Robert
   and Joanna Pond. She died March 6, 1756; and he died Sept. 6,
   1756, aged 73 years. They are buried at North Bellingham. He
   settled, soon after his marriage, in Wrentham, where he afterwards
   lived. He accumulated considerable property, as is shown by his
   will, and owned a negro slave. In his will, proved Oct. 8, 1756
   (Suffolk Co. Prob. Rec., vol. li., p. 781), he mentions children of
   his deceased daughters Anna Thayer and Esther Thayer; and his
   children Elizabeth Hayward, John Partridge, Keziah Thayer, and
   Sarah Adams. He also refers by name to his grandchildren John
   Partridge, Chloe Thayer, and Anna Rexford, wife of William Rexford. Of his children, the oldest was born in Medfield, the others
   in Wrentham.

   Children :

i. ANNA,[4] b. Dec. 14, 1709; m. Jan. 19, 1731, Nathaniel, b. Mendon,
  Apr. 20, 1708, son of Isaac and Mary Thayer, of Mendon. They
  resided in Mendon. Children.
ii. ELIZABETH, b. Dec., 1711; m. March 15, 1734, Samuel Hayward of
  Bellingham, where they resided. Several children.
19. iii. JOHN, b. June 2, 1715; d. Dec. 21, 1791.
iv. ESTHER, b. March 15, 1717; m. Feb. 10, 1734, Daniel Thayer of
  Bellingham. They settled in "the Gore," Oxford (now Charlton).
  Several children.
v. KEZIAH, m. Dec. 24, 1739, Samuel, b. Mendon, 1713, son of Isaac
  and Mary Thayer, of Mendon. They resided in Mendon. Children.
vi. SARAH, b. July 25, 1725; d. April 27, 1817; m. Dec. 25, 1744, Obadiah,
  b. Medway, Dec. 18, 1721, d. Jan. 2, 1803, son of Obadiah and
  Christian (Sanford) Adams. They resided in Bellingham. (See
  Adams Gen.) Children.

7. BENONI[3] PARTRIDGE (*John*,[2] *John*[1]) was born in Medfield (now
   Millis), May 25, 1687. He was one of the proprietors of the town
   of Medway at its incorporation, in 1713, and took up his residence
   in the new grant, now West Medway (Jameson's Hist. of Medway,
   p. 45). His children were born there. At his death, his farm was
   divided equally between his sons Timothy and Moses. He was a
   member of the First Church of Medway. He married, July 14,
   1708, Mehetabel, born in Medfield, Sept. 10, 1689, daughter of
   Samuel and Sarah (Kendrick) Wheelock, and grand-daughter of
   Ralph Wheelock, the founder of Medfield. She died Jan. 20, 1761;
   and he died Dec. 26, 1769.

Children :

20. 1. PRESERVED,[4] b. March 13, 1709.
    ii. THOMAS, b. Nov. 28, 1711; no further record.
    iii. SETH, b. March 17, 1713; d. Aug. 5, 1786; m. Ruth Holbrook, of
        Medway, who d. May 27, 1789, aged 77. No children.
21. iv. JOSEPH, b. Aug. 22, 1715; d. in 1753.
    v. DAVID, b. May 22, 1718; d. March 16, 1742.
    vi. MEHETABEL, b. April 24, 1720; d. Aug. 4, 1741.
    vii. SAMUEL, b. June 24, 1722; d. Sept. 7, 1741.
    viii. SARAH, b. Sept. 27, 1724; m. March 24, 1756, Samuel, b. Wenham,
        Feb. 14, 1728, d. Sept. 25, 1797, son of Daniel and Sarah (Fuller)
        Fiske. They resided in Upton and Shelburne, Mass. (See Fiske
        Gen.) Children.
22. ix. TIMOTHY, b. Jan. 18, 1727; d. Sept. 18, 1787.
23. x. ELI, b. June 3, 1729.
24. xi. MOSES, b. Aug. 28, 1733; d. Oct. 6, 1804.

8. JONATHAN[3] PARTRIDGE (*John*[2], *John*[1]) was born in Medfield (now
    Millis), Nov. 25, 1693. He drew land in Medway in 1713, and
    was selectman there in 1738. His farm lay about a mile north of
    Medway village. In 1742, he sold this place to his brother James,
    and removed to Sherborn. He resided there about ten years, and
    then removed to Barre, Rutland District, where he died about 1758.
    He married three times: first, Nov. 13, 1717, Elizabeth, born in
    Framingham, July 27, 1696, daughter of Isaac and Sarah (Bigelow)
    Learned. She died April 23, 1738; and he married second, Jan.
    18, 1739, Anne, daughter of John Phipps of Wrentham, and grand-
    niece of Sir William Phipps, Governor of Massachusetts (Morse's
    Hist. of Sherborn, p. 196). She died Feb. 9, 1749; and he mar-
    ried third, Oct. 12, 1749, Abigail Lovet of Medway. An order
    issued by the Judge of Probate for Worcester county, to the admin-
    istrator of his estate, refers to the "children of the deceased, being
    eighteen in number." The names of these children were endorsed
    on the back of the administrator's account (Worcester Prob., case
    45567). Thirteen were born in Medway, five in Sherborn, and two
    in Barre.

    Children by first wife :

    i. MARTHA,[4] b. March 16, 1718; m. 1740, John, b. Medfield, 1713, son
        of Henry and Elizabeth (Hilliard) Hooker (also spelled Hucker).
        They resided in Medfield, Medway and Rutland. One or more chil-
        dren.
    ii. ELIZABETH, b. Aug. 17, 1720; m. (1) Samuel, b. Sherborn, Aug. 11,
        1710, d. May 8, 1761, son of John and Hannah (Rockwood) Hill;
        m. (2) Nov. 27, 1771, Joseph Daniels of Needham. Children.
    iii. HULDAH, b. July 18, 1722; m. Oct. 22, 1740, Joseph, b. Sherborn,
        Apr. 1, 1701, son of Ebenezer and Mary (White) Hill. They re-
        sided in Holliston, where he d. May 23, 1767. Children.
25. iv. JONATHAN, b. July 16, 1724.
    v. MARY, b. July 19, 1726; m. Dec. 27, 1748, Thomas, b. Medway, April
        5, 1726, d. Dec. 5, 1773, son of Daniel and Sarah (Sanford) Adams.
        They resided in Medway. (See Adams Gen.) Children.
    vi. EDE, b. April 15, 1727; m. Jan. 18, 1750, Nathan, b. Medfield, Dec. 3,
        1724, son of Ebenezer and Susannah Bullard. They resided in
        Medfield and Shrewsbury. Children.
    vii. HANNAH, b. Feb. 12, 1729; m. March 7, 1751, Simon, b. Sherborn, Aug.
        21, 1730, d. May 10, 1790, son of William and Mehetabel (Breck)
        Leland. They resided in Sherborn. (See Leland Magazine.) Chil-
        dren.
26. viii. JASPER, b. April 15, 1732.

ix. LEARNED, b. Feb. 7, 1735; d. young.
27. x. SILAS, b. July 22, 1737.

Children by second wife:

28. xi. THADDEUS, b. Nov. 28, 1739.
29. xii. REUBEN, b. Nov. 21, 1741; d. Aug. 21, 1801.
xiii. JABEZ, b. Nov. 21, 1741; d. young.
xiv. RHODA, b. Feb. 11, 1744; m. Aug. 11, 1763, Samuel Cobb. They resided in Holliston. Children.
30. xv. JOHN, b. Oct. 28, 1746.
31. xvi. JABEZ, b. Dec. 11, 1748.

Children by third wife:

32. xvii. LOVET, b. Sept. 13, 1750.
33. xviii. STEPHEN, b. Aug. 2, 1752.
xix. ABIGAIL, b. Aug. 1, 1754; m. Sept. 22, 1774, Grindall, b. Mendon, Nov. 28, 1753, son of Seth and Anna Taft. One or more children.
34. xx. AMARIAH, b. May 21, 1756.

9. JAMES³ PARTRIDGE (*John,² John¹*) was born in Medfield (now Millis), Oct. 8, 1700. He resided in Medway, where his children were born. He was in the Colonial service in 1722. In 1742, he purchased his brother Jonathan's farm near Medway village. He married, Jan. 27, 1729, Keziah, born in Medway, Dec. 2. 1711, daughter of Malachi and Bethia (Fisher) Bullard. She died July 25, 1799; and he died March 9, 1769. In his will, which was dated April 23, 1762, he mentions his sons James, Malachi, Eleazer, Stephen, Joel and Nathan; and his daughters Keziah Thompson, Lois Pond, Bethia Hixon, Elizabeth, Lydia and Chloe. The valuation of his estate was £509. 14s. 2d. (Suffolk Co. Prob. Rec., vol. lxviii., p. 19).
Children :

35. i. JAMES,⁴ b. Oct. 10, 1730.
36. ii. MALACHI, b. Nov. 30, 1731.
iii. KEZIAH, b. Nov. 12, 1733; m. Lieut. Moses, b. Medway, Dec. 23, 1728, son of Eleazer and Hannah Thompson. They resided in West Medway, where she d. Oct. 31, 1784; and he d. June 24, 1794. Children.
iv. ASA, b. March 6, 1735; d. April 28, 1759.
v. LOIS, b. Sept. 20, 1736; m. July 29, 1756, Benjamin, b. Wrentham, March 21, 1731, son of Ichabod and Milcah (Farrington) Pond. He d. Dec. 27, 1809. They resided in Wrentham (now Franklin). (See Pond Gen.) Children.
vi. BETHIA, b. Nov. 22, 1738; m. March 15, 1759, Seth, b. Stoughton, 1734, son of Walter and Mary (Morse) Hixon. He d. July 13, 1821; and she d. Sept. 5, 1818. They resided in Medway. Children.
37. vii. ELEAZER, b. April 19, 1740; d. March 19, 1834.
viii. LYDIA, b. Dec. 6, 1743; m. Samuel, b. Holliston, Sept. 5, 1742, d. Jan. 27, 1816, son of Capt. Samuel and Deborah (Morse) Bullard. They resided in Holliston. Children.
38. ix. STEPHEN, b. June 10, 1746; d. June 14, 1818.
39. x. JOEL, b. Feb. 19, 1748; d. Feb. 13, 1823.
xi. EUNICE, b. July 26, 1749; d. young.
40. xii. NATHAN, b. March 26, 1751; d. May 25, 1785.
xiii. HANNAH, b. Sept. 19, 1753; d. Dec. 25, 1756.
xiv. ELIZABETH, d. Sept. 18, 1818; unmarried.
xv. CHLOE, b. April 11, 1756.

10. STEPHEN³ PARTRIDGE (*John,² John¹*) was born in Medfield (now Millis), April 16, 1706. He inherited his father's homestead in East Medway; and a barn supposed to have been built by him in 1740 is still standing. He married, April 7, 1737. Mary, born in Wrentham, May 25, 1710, daughter of Daniel and Mary (Heaton)

Maccane. He died March 10, 1742 ; and she married second, July 23, 1747, Abner Ellis.

Children :

i. MARY,[4] b. June 20, 1738; m. 1760, Joseph, b. Medfield, 1734, son of John and Rebecca (Fisher) Baxter, of Medfield. They resided in Medfield and Princeton. Four children.

ii. AZUBA, b. April 16, 1742; m. Dec. 25, 1765, Capt. Aaron, b. Sherborn, April 1, 1741, son of Addington Gardner of Sherborn. They resided in Sherborn. Six children.

11. ELEAZER[3] PARTRIDGE (*Eleazer,[2] John[1]*) was born in Medfield, March 7, 1693. He settled in that portion of Dedham which, in 1724, became Walpole. Of the births of his children, three are recorded in Medfield, three in Dedham, and that of the youngest in Walpole. He married twice: first, April 11, 1715, Sarah Taylor, who died Feb., 1758; and second, Nov. 20, 1759, Ruth, born in Wrentham, Oct. 14, 1720, daughter of Ebenezer and Bethia Ware. He died in 1776, and his will, proved May 6, 1776, mentions his wife Ruth ; sons Elisha and Henry; and daughters Sarah Blanchard and Elizabeth Morse (Suffolk Co. Prob. Rec., vol. lxxv., p. 161).

Children :

41. i. ELISHA,[4] b. March 6, 1716.

ii. ELEAZER, b. Nov. 17, 1717; d. May 6, 1752; m. Nov. 25, 1741, Jemima Clark. She m. (2) Oct. 9, 1755, John Fisher of Wrentham. No children.

iii. SARAH, b. April 6, 1719; m. Jan. 2, 1744, Stephen Blanchard.

iv. ELIZABETH, b. June 4, 1721; m. Jan. 3, 1740, Timothy, Jr., b. Dedham, April 8, 1716, son of Timothy and Mehetabel (Robbins) Morse. They resided in Stoughton. The Morse Memorial, p. 48, errs in saying she d. before 1764, and that her husband m. (2) Nov. 28, 1764, Lydia Fisher. She was living in 1776, as shown by her father's will. Her son, Timothy Morse, 3d, b. April 23, 1741, was probably the Timothy who m. Lydia Fisher. (See Morse Memoir.)

v. PETER, b. May 16, 1722; prob. d. young.

42. vi. HENRY, b. Sept. 6, 1724.

vii. EZRA, b. May 17, 1734; d. June 10, 1734.

12. JOB[3] PARTRIDGE (*Eleazer,[2] John[1]*) was born in Medfield, May 19, 1698. He was in the Colonial service in 1722. He married twice: first, in 1724, Abigail, born in Medfield, July 23, 1704, died in Wrentham, April 1, 1728, daughter of Ebenezer and Susannah Thompson ; and second, Feb. 28, 1729, Anne Cook of Bellingham. He was drowned at Wrentham, Feb. 7, 1742. His widow was administratrix of his estate, which was valued at £641. 11s. (Suffolk Co. Prob. Rec., vol. xxxvi., p. 157). She died Nov. 24, 1752,

Child by first wife :

i. BENONI,[4] b. March 24, 1726; d. 1747, at Cape Breton.

Children by second wife :

ii. JOB, b. April 24, 1730; d. Jan. 22, 1742.

iii. ANNE, b. April 3, 1731; d. in infancy.

iv. ANNE, b. Feb. 19, 1733; d. May 27, 1756; m. March 26, 1755, at Cumberland, R. I., Cornelius Cook of Wrentham. One child.

v. RHODA, b. April 8, 1734; d. Jan. 6, 1742.

vi. SETH, b. March 20, 1736. A Seth Partridge, of Wrentham, m. Oct. 9, 1760, Mercy Harding of Medway.

43. vii. LEVI, b. Sept. 22, 1739; d. Jan. 29, 1813.

13. JOSEPH[3] PARTRIDGE (*Eleazer,*[2] *John*[1]) was born in Medfield, March 15, 1706. He removed with his father to Bellingham, where he afterwards resided. He married twice: first, Feb. 26, 1729, Elizabeth (or Betty), born in Medfield (now Medway), Nov. 10, 1705, daughter of Henry and Sarah (Wheelock) Guernsey (spelled Garnsey). She died in Bellingham, Jan. 13, 1732; and he married second, Dec. 21, 1732, Eunice, born in Sherborn, Aug. 10, 1706, daughter of Jonathan and Jane (Whitney) Morse. She died Nov. 3, 1785, "aged 80 years" (Bellingham Town Records); and he died June 22, 1770, "aged 65 years." Aaron Holbrook, of Bellingham, was admitted administrator on his estate, July 13, 1770 (Suffolk Co. Prob. Rec., vol. lxix, p. 164). In the final settlement of the estate the widow Eunice received one third and her son-in-law, Aaron Holbrook, the remaining two thirds, the latter paying to Joseph's only surviving child, Elizabeth, and to the children of his deceased daughter, Keziah Hill, their ratable shares.

Children by first wife:

i. KEZIAH,[4] b. Jan. 22, 1730; d. Nov. 7, 1767; m. March 18, 1758, Ephraim, b. Wrentham, July 10, 1731, son of Ebenezer and Ann (Allen) Hill. They resided in West Medway. Children.
ii. ELIZABETH, b. Dec. 24, 1731; d. Feb. 4, 1772; unmarried.

Children by second wife:

iii. HANNAH, b. Nov. 6, 1733; m. June 23, 1762, Aaron, b. Bellingham, Aug. 31, 1730, son of John and Hannah Holbrook. Children. They resided in Bellingham. He d. April 4, 1818.
iv. ASA, b. Oct. 23, 1736; d. young.
v. RACHEL, b. May 14, 1739; d. young.
vi. PHEBE, b. July 2, 1741; d. young.
vii. JOSEPH, b. May 26, 1743; d. Oct. 7, 1746.
viii. PETER, b. July 17, 1745; d. Oct. 8, 1746.
ix. RHODA, b. Oct. 17, 1748; d. Feb. 20, 1751.

14. BENJAMIN[3] PARTRIDGE (*Eleazer,*[2] *John*[1]) was born in Medfield, May 16, 1713. He accompanied his father to Bellingham, where he thereafter resided. He married, Sept. 13, 1737, Sarah, born in Medfield, Nov. 24, 1716, daughter of James and Rebecca (Turner) Allen. She died Sept. 4, 1801; and he died Feb. 10, 1805.

Children:

i. LOIS,[4] b. June 24, 1738; d. July 8, 1738.
44. ii. BENJAMIN, b. Oct. 24, 1739; d. Sept. 16, 1776.
45. iii. JOB, b. Feb. 28, 1741; d. Sept. 10, 1823.
iv. SARAH, b. April 10, 1744; d. July 12, 1831; m. (published Dec. 1, 1771) Billy, b. Wrentham, March 21, 1743, d. Aug. 22, 1821, son of Eleazer and Hannah Ware. They resided in Franklin. Children.
46. v. JOSEPH, b. July 24, 1747; d. May 24, 1810.
vi. SIMEON, b. Jan. 2, 1749; d. Oct. 5, 1761.
vii. AARON, b. Oct. 28, 1752: d. Oct. 18, 1761.

15. ZACHARIAH[3] PARTRIDGE (*Eleazer,*[2] *John*[1]) was born in Medfield, March 22, 1720. He settled in Walpole. His father referred to him in his will as "my son, being yet young," and desired that he be apprenticed "to such trade as he may choose." He was also to receive £10 upon becoming of age (Suffolk Co. Prob. Rec., vol. xxxiii., p. 5). He married in Walpole, Feb. 17, 1742, Esther, daughter of Ebenezer and Esther (Clark) Turner, of Medfield. They resided in Walpole, and their children were born there. "Mer-

cy, wife of Zachariah Partridge, died Apr. 25, 1798." (Walpole Records.) No record of a second marriage has yet been found. He died Feb. 7, 1799.

Children:

47. i. ZACHARIAH,[4] b. Jan. 15, 1744.
ii. ESTHER, bapt. Jan. 15, 1746; d. Feb. 21, 1750.
48. iii. JESSE, b. Feb. 28, 1748; d. March 29, 1838.
iv. A SON (name torn in record), b. May 7, 1750.
v. ESTHER, b. Aug. 9, 1752.
vi. ABEL, b. Oct. 31, 1754; d. Sept. 19, 1757.
vii. DANIEL, b. Feb. 23, 1757; d. Sept. 24, 1757.
viii. SETH, b. March 20, 1759; no further record.
ix. PETER, b. May 21, 1761; d. Feb. 19, 1778, in camp (Mass. Archives).

16. SAMUEL[3] PARTRIDGE (*Samuel,*[2] *John*[1]) was born in Medfield (now Rockville), Nov. 6, 1704. He settled in Wrentham (now Franklin), where his children were born. He married, Dec. 28, 1736, Mary Blood. She died July 29, 1775. He died before Dec. 8, 1774, for on that date an agreement among his heirs, relating to the division of his estate, was filed in the probate office at Boston (Suffolk Co. Prob. Rec., vol. lxxx., p. 266).

Children:

49. i. SAMUEL,[4] b. Mch. 31, 1741; d. Nov. 9, 1776.
50. ii. AMOS, b. July 25, 1742.
51. iii. REUBEN, b. Apr. 14, 1744.
iv. MARY, b. Aug. 8, 1745; m. Mch. 5, 1764, Jonathan Hawes, of Wrentham. They resided in Wrentham (now Franklin). Children.
v. SILENCE, b. Mch. 9, 1747; d. young.
vi. RHODA, b. Apr. 9, 1748; m. May 30, 1764, Samuel Goldsbury, of Wrentham.
vii. DAVID, b. July 22, 1750; d. Nov., 1781.
viii. ELIZABETH, b. Oct. 8, 1752; m. ——— Daniels.

17. EBENEZER[3] PARTRIDGE (*Samuel,*[2] *John*[1]) was born in Medfield (now Rockville), May 29, 1706. He settled in Wrentham (now Franklin), where he afterwards resided. He married in Walpole, Nov. 5, 1735, Elizabeth Holmes. ·She died Oct. 6, 1784. He died May 15, 1794 (Diary of Mercy and Lucina Wight, of Bellingham). In consideration of £200 he conveyed, April 24, 1773, to David and Hannah Wood, one half part of all his lands and buildings in Wrentham (Suffolk Co. Deeds, Lib. cxxv., p. 225). In a deed dated June 5, 1789, one hundred and forty acres of land in Franklin is conveyed to "my son-in-law David Wood and Hannah, his wife, my daughter" (Suffolk Co. Deeds, Lib. clxvi., p. 233).

Children:

i. ELIZABETH,[4] b. Aug. 28, 1737; d. Jan. 27, 1749.
ii. HANNAH, b. May 1, 1741; m. (pub. Walpole, Mch. 24, 1771) David Wood. They resided in Franklin. Children.
iii. ABIGAIL, b. Aug. 29, 1744; m. July 16, 1767 (pub. Walpole, June 21, 1767), Elkanah, b. Walpole, Oct. 2, 1740, d. Mansfield, Oct. 13, 1805, son of Joshua and Abigail (Bullard) Clapp. They resided in Mansfield. Five children. (See Clapp Gen.)

18. JOSHUA[3] PARTRIDGE (*Samuel,*[2] *John*[1]) was born in Medway (now Rockville), July 27, 1713. He purchased property near his father's place in Medway, lying along the banks of Charles River (Suffolk Co. Deeds, Libs. liii., p. 40; lix., p. 37; lxxxix., pp. 190 to 197).

He resided there during his life, and upon his death bequeathed the homestead to his son Samuel. He served several terms on the board of selectmen of Medway. He was in the Colonial service in 1754, 1756 and 1758 (Jameson's Hist. of Medway, p. 213). He was chosen captain of the "First. Military Company" of Medway, which saw frequent service during the Revolution. He married, Dec. 23, 1742, Elizabeth, born in Wrentham, Nov. 10, 1718, daughter of Daniel and Elizabeth (Stevens) Kingsbury. He died Jan. 19, 1795.

Children:

    i. ELIZABETH,⁴ b. Sept. 28, 1743; d. Jan. 3, 1744.
52. ii. JOSHUA, b. Apr. 20, 1745; d. Aug. 15, 1802.
    iii. ELIZABETH, b. Mch. 20, 1747; m. (1) Nov. 27, 1766, John Wheeler. According to Jameson, she m. (2) Ira Richardson, (3) Asaph Leland, and (4) Joseph Lovell, although he wrongly gives Richardson as her first husband.
    iv. ICHABOD, b. Aug. 13, 1749; d. Apr. 11, 1764.
53. v. SAMUEL, b. Dec. 26, 1752; d. Feb. 17, 1842.
    vi. RHODA, b. Feb. 3, 1759.

19. JOHN⁴ PARTRIDGE (*John,³ John,² John¹*) was born in Wrentham, June 2, 1715. He divided with his son John most of his father's real estate, and was executor of the latter's will (Suffolk Co. Prob. Rec., vol. li., p. 781). He married twice: first, Nov. 10, 1737, Abigail Thayer, born in Mendon, Aug. 22, 1718, daughter of Samuel and Mary (Sampson) Thayer. She died March 11, 1774, and he married second, Dec. 8, 1774, Catharine Holbrook of Mendon, who survived him. He died Dec. 21, 1791. John Allen, of Franklin, was admitted administrator on his estate, April 17, 1792 (Suffolk Co. Prob. Rec., vol. xci., p. 272). The total valuation of his real and personal property was £730. 7s. 5d. He resided in Wrentham (now Franklin), where his children were born.

Children:

    i. JOHN,⁵ b. Oct. 16, 1738; m. June 2, 1763, Abigail, b. Holliston, July, 1741, dau. of Samuel and Dinah (White) Leland. He d. May 14, 1764; and she d. May 26, 1764. No children.
    ii. ASA, b. July 24, 1740; d. Dec. 10, 1746.
    iii. JOSEPH, b. Oct. 26, 1742; d. Oct. 10, 1746.
    iv. SAMUEL, b. Apr. 15, 1744; d. Apr. 15, 1744.
    v. STEPHEN, b. Apr. 15, 1744; d. Apr. 15, 1744.
    vi. ABIGAIL, b. Oct, 26, 1745; d. Feb. 20, 1746.
    vii. MICAH, b. Dec. 20, 1746; d. Dec. 20, 1746.
    viii. ABIGAIL, b. Jan. 23, 1754; m. July 11, 1771, John Allen of Wrentham (now Franklin), where they resided. She d. Feb. 3, 1815; and he d. July 24, 1815. Several children, among whom *Ellery Allen*, b. Mch. 10, 1783, m. Dec. 2, 1800, Experience⁵ Partridge, dau. of Job⁴ (45).

20. PRESERVED⁴ PARTRIDGE (*Benoni,³ John,² John¹*) was born in Medfield (now West Medway), March 13, 1709. He married, Nov. 10, 1737, Catharine Armstrong, and soon after settled in Holliston. He was also in Milford as early as 1750, and as late as 1754 (Ballou's Hist. of Milford). He was in the Colonial service in 1755 (Mass. Archives). He removed as early as 1761 to Cumberland County, Maine, settling near Gorham. Two daughters were married at Gorham before 1766. In 1764 the parish of Stroudwater (now a suburb of Portland) was incorporated, and his name

appears in the assessors' book for that year as a tax payer. (Letter, dated Jan. 31, 1902, from Leonard B. Chapman, Portland, Me).

Children:

i. NATHAN,[5] b. Aug. 3, 1738; d. in Westbrook, Me., 1786; settled in Falmouth, Me., 1761; in Revolutionary service, 1775-1780; m. Jan. 1, 1781, Anne, dau. of Samuel and Mary (Peabody) Conant, of Falmouth. They resided in Saccarappa (now Westbrook), Me. Children: 1. *Nancy,*[6] b. Aug. 27, 1781; d. Sept. 17, 1873; m. Feb. 21, 1802, Josiah, b. Windham, Me., Mch. 31, 1773, d. Casco, Me., Jan. 3, 1834, son of William and Mary (Westcott) Maxfield; resided in Casco, Me.; nine children. 2. *Catharine*, b. July 18, 1783; d. Jan. 10, 1861; m. 1803, Daniel Dole, b. Newbury, Mass., Aug. 26, 1757, d. Stroudwater, Me., Feb. 23, 1815; resided in Stroudwater; five children. 3. *Joseph*, b. Apr. 13, 1785; d. Sept. 27, 1856; m. Apr. 13, 1808, Lydia Quinby, b. Somersworth, N. H., Mch. 15, 1787; resided in Westbrook, Me. Twelve children.

ii. BATHSHEBA, b. Aug. 19, 1740; m. (pub. Gorham, Oct. 16, 1761) Uriah, son of Richard Nason of Gorham, Me., who d. May 13, 1833, aged 91. They resided in Gorham and Poland, Me. Several children.

iii. JESSE, b. Aug. 29, 1742; d. Dec. 21, 1795. He was engaged in trading at Falmouth, Me., and owned considerable real estate. He was in Revolutionary service, and commissioned captain, Apr. 9, 1778 (Mass. Archives). He m. (1) Lydia, dau. of John and Jane (Brady) Bailey, of Falmouth. (L. B. Chapman, in Me. Hist. Soc. Coll., 2d series, vol. x., p. 298; also confirmed by Jesse's grandniece, Miss Emma Partridge, of Portland, Me.) She apparently d. before him, for his widow, Rebecca Partridge, received a third of his real estate (Cumberland Co. Deeds). The widow Rebecca m. later Andrew Titcomb. No children by either wife.

iv. CATHARINE, b. Aug. 26, 1744; d. Mch. 24, 1832; m. 1766, Timothy, b. Presumscot Lower Falls, Me., 1737, d. Oct. 22, 1829, son of Edward and Sarah (Collins) Cloudman. They resided in Gorham, Me. Eleven children.

v. DAVID, b. Jan. 26, 1747; settled at Falmouth, Me., where he m. Mary, b. there, May, 1749, dau. of Samuel and Mary (Peabody) Conant. He was in Revolutionary service, and was for a short time held prisoner by the British (Mass. Archives). He resided at Saccarappa (Falmouth), now Westbrook, Me., until about 1790, when he removed to Thompson's Pond (now West Poland), Me., where he d. Mch. 22, 1834. His widow d. there, Apr. 29, 1847. (Poole's Hist. Poland, Me.) His children were: 1. *David*,[6] b. 1773; d. Dec. 3, 1858; m. Rebecca, b. 1774, d. June 25, 1851, dau. of John Wooster; resided in W. Poland, Me.; nine children. 2. *Polly*, m. —— Bartlett; resided in Gorham, Me. 3. *Daniel*, d. young. 4. *Eunice*, m. William Pride; resided in Westbrook. 5. *Samuel*, m. Thankful Baker; resided in Poland; nine children. 6. *Catharine*, b. Jan. 4, 1791; d. May 1, 1887; m. Mch., 1822, George, b. at Gorham, Nov. 14, 1779, d. at W. Poland, Oct. 29, 1868, son of Moses Hanscomb; resided in W. Poland; one son. 7. *Nathan*, b. Feb. 15, 1793; d. Mch. 30, 1850; m. Mch. 17, 1822, Nancy Pitcher, b. Andover, Mass., Oct. 3, 1799, d. Apr. 6, 1887; resided in Boston; seven children.

vi. JOTHAM, bapt. July 27, 1750; settled at Falmouth, Me. He was in the Revolution (Mass. Archives). He m. a dau. of John and Jane (Brady) Bailey, of Falmouth. (Statement of his grand niece, Miss Emma Partridge, of Portland, Me.) They resided in Westbrook. He conveyed property to his son *Jotham*,[6] *Jr.*, Oct. 22, 1800 (Cumberland Co. Deeds, vol. xxxv., p. 13). He probably also had a son *Nathaniel*.

vii. AZUBA, bapt. Dec. 18, 1752; m. Joseph Quinby of Falmouth, Me., where they lived. He d. between Apr. 9, 1798, and Jan. 3, 1800.

viii. ROSINA, m. Nathan Quinby of Falmouth, where they resided.

ix. ZIPPORAH, b. 1757; m. Eliphalet, b, Gorham, Me., Mch. 20, 1759, son of Eliphalet and Elizabeth (Phinney) Watson. They resided in Waterford, Me. Children.

x. RHODA, contributed to Congregational Church of Westbrook, Me., June 24, 1799. Never married.

21. JOSEPH[4] PARTRIDGE (*Benoni*,[3] *John*,[2] *John*[1]) was born in West Medway, Aug. 22, 1715. He married, Feb. 11, 1747, Mary, daughter of Nathaniel and Mary Sheffield, of Sherborn. They resided in Holliston, where he died before March 6, 1754. His widow was admitted administratrix on his estate, April 15, 1754. His real and personal property were appraised at £1800 (Middlesex Co. Prob., case 12080). His widow married second, Dec. 4, 1755, James Torrey of Upton. In 1758, a petition signed by Preserved, Timothy, Moses, Jesse, Eli, Rachel and Katherine Partridge, was presented to the Judge of Probate for Middlesex County, to have Mary Torrey dismissed as guardian of her two children, and to have their uncle Seth Partridge appointed in her stead, it having been represented that the father-in-law (Torrey) was attempting to get possession of the children's property (Middlesex Co. Prob., case 12080).

Children:

i. URANIA,[5] b. Oct. 7, 1750.
ii. ANNA. An Ann Partridge of Medway, m. May 1, 1771, Jonathan Holbrook of Bellingham.

22. TIMOTHY[4] PARTRIDGE (*Benoni*,[3] *John*,[2] *John*[1]) was born in West Medway, Jan. 18, 1727. He married, Jan. 15, 1755, Abigail, born in Medway, March 27, 1732, daughter of Joseph and Abigail (Hawes) Barber. She died Feb. 22, 1809. He received one half of his father's homestead in West Medway, where he always resided. He was in the Colonial and Revolutionary service (Mass. Archives). He died Sept. 18, 1787; and his will, proved Oct. 2, 1787, names his widow Abigail, his sons Samuel and Elijah, and his daughter Eunice Mann (Suffolk Co. Probate Rec., vol. lxxxvi., p. 523).

Children:

i. SAMUEL,[5] b. Mch. 18, 1756; d. Mch. 29, 1832; m. June 5, 1782, Elizabeth McIntyre of Needham, b. Oct. 11, 1759, d. Jan. 12, 1830. They settled in Paxton. Children: 1. *Abigail*[6] (*Nabby*), b. Nov. 14, 1782. 2. *Silence*, b. Oct. 9, 1784. 3. *Zillah*, b. May 27, 1786. 4. *Polly*, b. May 11, 1789; m. Clarke Pike. 5. *Betsey*, b. Nov. 11, 1791. 6. *David*, b. Mch. 31, 1795; d. Apr. 19, 1850; m. Sarah Haskell of Barre, b. Jan. 20, 1799, d. Sept. 26, 1884; resided at Paxton until 1843, when he removed to Worcester; six children. 7. *John*, b. June 1, 1799; d. July 30, 1872; resided in Paxton; three children. 8. *Sarah*, b. Jan. 9, 1801.
ii. EUNICE, b. Mch. 15, 1758; d. Oct. 9, 1828; m. Mch. 6, 1783, Ralph Mann of Walpole. He d. May 12, 1820, aged 92.
iii. ELIJAH, b. Apr. 4, 1762; d. Sept. 9, 1805; inherited his father's homestead in W. Medway, and resided there. He m. (1) Keziah W. Curtis, who d. Jan. 16, 1795; m. (2) Catharine Clark who d. June 18, 1834. Children: 1. *Rachel*,[6] b. Dec. 7, 1785; m. Daniel Leland, Jr., of Sherborn. 2. *Leah*, b. Jan. 7, 1788; d. Jan. 9, 1788. 3. *Timothy*, b. Mch. 14, 1789; d. June 13, 1827; m. Charlotte, dau. of Jonathan Adams, who d. Dec. 4, 1834, in Medway, where they resided; seven children. 4. *Clark*, b. May 16, 1799. 5. *Catharine*, b. Feb. 6, 1801. 6. *Elijah*, b. Jan. 29, 1805; m. (1) Dec. 11, 1839,

Ruth, dau. of Jotham Adams, who was b. Aug. 19, 1811, and d. Jan. 29, 1856; m. (2) Oct. 3, 1867, Lucy G. Dodge, b. Burnham, Mc., Mch. 25, 1832; resided in Medway; one child by second wife.

iv. ZILLAH, b. Mch. 12, 1764; d. Oct. 12, 1783.

v. DAVID, b. Dec. 30, 1765; d. Sept. 25, 1783.

23. ELI[4] PARTRIDGE (*Benoni,*[3] *John,*[2] *John*[1]) was born in West Medway, June 3, 1729. He married Rachel, born March 30, 1732, daughter of Nathaniel and Mary Sheffield, of Sherborn. He settled in Holliston about 1751 or 1752, but soon removed to Milford (Ballou's Hist. of Milford). In 1754 he purchased a place in Mendon, and removed there. He was in the Colonial service in 1745 (Mass. Archives). In 1761 he sold his right to a 60-acre lot of land in the township of New Boston, Cumberland Co. (Maine), which was to be drawn for him by the proprietors of said township (Cumberland Co. Deeds, vol. i., p. 154). In 1776 he sold his Mendon property, and removed with his family to Chesterfield, N. H. (Randall's History of Chesterfield.) He died in Littleton, N. H., after 1800. His oldest child was born in Holliston; the next ten in Mendon. The statement by Randall that he had a son Adam may be on authority of tradition.

Children:

i. SHEFFIELD,[5] b. Nov. 2, 1752; was in Revolutionary service from Mendon (Mass. Archives). He is said to have removed to Ohio after 1800. (Letter, dated Nov. 24, 1875, from his nephew, Benjamin F. Partridge of DePeyster, N. Y.)

ii. JOSEPH, b. June 30, 1754; m. Nov. 15, 1778, Sarah, b. in Milford, Oct. 8, 1759, dau. of Capt. Samuel and Eunice (Corbett) Warren. He was in Revolutionary service, from Milford (Mass. Archives). They resided in Milford until 1781, when they removed to Chesterfield, N. H., where they afterwards lived (Randall's Hist. of Chesterfield). He d. in 1817; and she d. in 1849. Children: 1. *Caroline,*[6] b. May 30, 1779; d. Sept. 15, 1787. 2. *Prusia,* b. Mch. 18, 1781; m. Alexander Albee; resided in Littleton, N. H.; children. 3. *John Warren,* b. Dec. 16, 1782; d. Feb. 7, 1865; m. Mch. 4, 1807, Mary, b. Westmoreland, N. H., Jan. 24, 1788, d. Nov. 23, 1869, dau. of Abiather and Mary Lincoln; settled in Peacham, Vt., soon after marriage, removing in 1811 to Burlington, Vt., where they afterwards lived; six children. 4. *Mehetabel,* b. Dec. 20, 1784; m. Calvin, son of Samuel and Sarah Gilson, of Chesterfield, N. H.; d. in 1857. 5. *Joseph,* b. Jan. 28, 1787; d. Sept. 29, 1873; m. in 1811, Catharine, b. Aug. 2, 1791, dau. of Capt. Simon and Mary Willard, of Chesterfield, who d. Feb. 3, 1865; resided a number of years in Peacham, Vt., then removed to Osceola, Stark Co., Ill., where they thereafter resided; six children. 6. *Lyman,* b. July 21, 1789; d. May 28, 1852; m. July 5, 1818, Theodosia Wood of Westmoreland, N. H., who was b. in 1794, and d. Jan. 25, 1866; resided in Peacham, Vt.; eight children. 7. *Winslow,* b. July 1, 1791; m. Lavernia Wood, of Westmoreland, N. H., sister of Lyman's wife; was a well-to-do manufacturer, of Watertown, N. Y., where he lived; children, but male line extinct. 8. *Sarah,* b. May 4, 1793; d. July 12, 1798. 9. *Abel,* b. May 17, 1795; m. Sylvia ———; resided in Highgate, Vt. 10. *Ora,* b. June 4, 1798; m. Betsey, dau. of Levi Ware of Westmoreland, N. H.; went to Covington, N. Y. 11. *Samuel J.,* b. Nov. 22, 1800; d. Apr. 30, 1884; m. Oct. 25, 1827, Lucretia, b. Nov. 9, 1801, dau. of Ziba and Nancy (Babbitt) Albee; resided in Chesterfield, N. H.; three children.

iii. ELI, b. Dec. 30, 1756; d. Nov. 3, 1792; was in Revolutionary service from Mendon (Mass. Archives), and from Chesterfield, N. H.

(Hammond's Rev. Rolls). They resided in Chesterfield. His wife's name was Persis. Children: 1. *Elkanah,*[6] b. Sept. 4, 1780; d. Mch. 3, 1858; m. Jan. 9, 1809, Sarah, daughter of William Lee, of Antwerp, N. Y., who was b. May 23, 1794, and d. Dec. 16, 1865; settled about 1811 in Dekalb, St. Lawrence Co., N. Y., removing later to Macomb, N. Y. (same county), where they afterwards lived; eleven children. 2. *Ira,* b. Mch. 22, 1783; d. in infancy. 3. *Ira,* b. July 19, 1785; went to Indiana after 1800, and d. there, unm., about 1817. 4. *Azubah,* b. Aug. 15, 1787; m. Joseph Hersey. 5. *Caroline,* b. Oct. 21, 1789; m. James Wood.

iv.   AMOS, b. Apr. 12, 1758; was in Revolutionary service from Mendon (Mass. Archives), and from Chesterfield, N. H. (Hammond's Rev. Rolls). He m. at Athol, Mass., Aug. 28, 1783, Sarah, b. Northfield, Mass., Nov. 9, 1764, dau. of Capt. Ebenezer and Sarah (Janes) Harvey, of Northfield, Mass., and later of Chesterfield, N. H. They resided in Athol until about 1800, thence removing to Chesterfield. He located at Peacham, Vt., about 1804, and at Keene, Essex Co., N. Y., before 1809. In 1826 they accompanied their son Benjamin F. Partridge to De Peyster, St. Lawrence Co., N. Y., where they thereafter resided. He d. at Ogdensburg, N. Y., Jan. 3, 1844; and she d. at De Peyster, N. Y., Aug. 23, 1849. Children: 1. *Hannah,*[6] b. Aug. 23, 1784; m. Lane Hurd, of Keene, N. Y.; children. 2. *James Oliver,* b. Mch. 3, 1786; d. July 11, 1869; resided in Jay, Essex Co., N. Y.; m. Experience Snow; children. 3. *Alpheus Moore,* b. Aug. 27, 1787; d. May 19, 1873; resided in Keene, N. Y.; children. 4. *Sarah,* b. July 26, 1789; d. Nov. 6, 1853; m. Dec. 16, 1814, Moses Hardy, b. Fryeburg, Me., Feb. 16, 1787, d. Mch. 3, 1869; settled at De Peyster, N. Y.; two children. 5. *Rachel,* b. Mch. 19, 1791; m. Benjamin Baxter; resided in Jay or Keene, N. Y.; no children. 6. *Polly,* b. Aug. 12, 1792; d. Nov. 12, 1847; m. Capt. John Finch of Keene, N. Y.; settled in 1826 at De Peyster, N. Y.; children. 7. *Amos,* b. June 11, 1794; d. Jan. 8, 1886; m. July 23, 1823, Abigail, b. July 30, 1800, d. Dec. 26, 1885, dau. of Capt. David and Mary (Chambers) Lewis, of Elizabethtown, N. Y.; settled in De Peyster, N. Y.; ten children. 8. *Betsey,* b. July 25, 1796; d. Feb. 23, 1875; m. July 23, 1823, Jared, b. Mch. 12, 1802, d. Dec. 5, 1855, son of Silas and Sarah (Smith) Thayer; resided in Wilmington, N. Y.; children. 9. *Sophronia,* b. April 17, 1798; d. Feb. 13, 1853; m. Adolphus, b. Pomfret, Conn., Nov. 1, 1796, d. Nov. 12, 1853, son of Thomas and Alithea (Smith) Ruggles; resided in Keene, Peru, Ogdensburg and Oswego, N. Y.; five children. 10. *Arathusa,* b. Feb. 27, 1800; d. in infancy. 11. *Eli,* b. Mch. 9, 1801; d. Oct. 22, 1811. 12. *Benjamin Franklin,* b. Sept. 17, 1803; m. Keene, N. Y., Apr. 6, 1826, Mary Howard, b. Mch. 9, 1804, d. Jan. 19, 1878, dau. of Artemas and Esther (Cragin) Wheeler, of Temple, N. H.; removed to De Peyster, St. Lawrence Co., N. Y., in 1826; resided there, where he d. Aug. 21, 1893; ten children. 13. *Arathusa,* b. Oct. 30, 1805; d. Mch. 13, 1891; m. in 1829, Adam, b. in Montrose, Susquehannah Co., Penn., son of Jacob and Elsie (Stawring) Fishbeck; resided in Macomb, N. Y.; eight children. 14. *Rufus Harvey,* b. Sept. 29, 1809; d. Nov. 29, 1844; m. Feb. 19, 1835, Mary L., b. Dec. 5, 1816, d. Dec. 27, 1894, dau. of Moses and Betsey (Davis) King, of De Peyster, N. Y., where they resided; two children; she m. (2) Marvel M. Church, of Baldwinsville, N.Y.

v.   MEHETABEL, b. July 7, 1759.

vi.   MARY, b. July 19, 1763; d. July 11, 1796; m. in 1780, Nathaniel, son of Lawrence Walton, of Chesterfield, N. H., where they resided, and he d. Apr. 25, 1817, aged 61. Children.

vii.   RACHEL, b. May 5, 1765; d. Jan. 11, 1840; m. in 1786, Rufus, b. Northfield, Mass., Feb. 22, 1763, d. May 29, 1840, son of Capt. Ebenezer and Sarah (Janes) Harvey. They resided in Chesterfield. Children.

viii.   NATHANIEL, bapt. Jan. 28, 1767; m. ——— Goodale, and removed to Littleton, N. H., where they lived. Several children.

ix.   JOHN, b. Apr. 2, 1770; no further record.

x. ABEL, bapt. June 30, 1776; drowned at Bellows Falls, Vt.
xi. CHARLES, b. Oct. 30, 1776; m. in 1800, Miriam Cunningham, and removed from Chesterfield to Ohio (letter, dated Nov. 24, 1875, from his nephew, Benj. F. Partridge).
xii. ADAM. No further record.

24. MOSES[4] PARTRIDGE (*Benoni,*[3] *John,*[2] *John*[1]) was born in West Medway, Aug. 28, 1733. He inherited one half of his father's homestead in West Medway, and resided there until 1801, when he sold the place to his son Simeon, and removed to Upton, where he died Oct. 6, 1804. He was in the Colonial and Revolutionary service (Mass. Archives). He married, Sept. 9, 1755, Rachel, daughter of Ziba Thayer of Uxbridge. She died Sept. 6, 1812.

Children:

i. FREELOVE,[5] b. Feb. 11, 1757; m. June 29, 1778, David Pike. They settled in Rockingham, Vt.
ii. SIMEON, b. Feb. 28, 1760; m. 1784, Jerusha White of Franklin. He resided in West Medway, where he d. Jan. 9, 1832. His widow d. Mch. 23, 1834. Children: 1. *Lyman,*[6] b. Nov. 21, 1785; d. Aug. 12, 1805, unmarried. 2. *Elihu,* b. Sept. 28, 1787; d. Oct. 13, 1848; m. (1) Nov. 7, 1810, Charlotte, b. Medway, June 17, 1788, d. Mch. 2, 1833, dau. of Dr. Aaron and Jemima Wight; m. (2) Mch. 13, 1834, Maria, dau. of Capt. William Paine of Wellfleet. Five children.
iii. BEULAH, b. July 5, 1762; m. Mch. 1858; m. (1) Dec. 8, 1782, Elias Hayward, who. d. Oct. 22, 1783; m. (2) June 26, 1788, Daniel Fiske of Upton.
iv. TABITHA, b. Apr. 30, 1765; m. July 5, 1801, James Johnson, and d. soon after.
v. CLARISSA, b. June 14, 1775; m. (1) Jan. 11, 1795, Gregory Ide, who d. Aug. 6, 1798; m. (2) Oct. 23, 1799, Asa Childs. She resided at Upton and Foxboro', and removed to Pittsburg, Pa.

25. JONATHAN[4] PARTRIDGE (*Jonathan,*[3] *John,*[2] *John*[1]) was born in Medway, July 16, 1724. He married, Feb. 6, 1756, at Barre, Keziah Hastings. Four children were born there; but nothing is learned of him or his family after 1764.

Children:

i. JONATHAN,[5] b. Feb. 21, 1757.
ii. JACOB, b. Dec. 12, 1759.
iii. KEZIAH, b. Apr. 29, 1761.
iv. LYDIA, b. July 14, 1764.

26. JASPER[4] PARTRIDGE (*Jonathan,*[3] *John,*[2] *John*[1]) was born in Medway, April 15, 1732. He married first, at Barre, Oct. 12, 1756, Mary, born May 18, 1737, daughter of Jonas and Jane (Hall) Rice, of Worcester, and settled soon after at Guilford, Vt., where he afterwards lived. His first wife died in 1767; and he married second, ———— Nichols, of Guilford.

Children by first wife:

i. JONAS.[5]
ii. THOMAS, removed to Boylstown, Oswego Co., N. Y., before 1786; later settled in Western Pennsylvania, and finally at Gustavus, Trumbull Co., Ohio, where he d. aged 70. Children: 1. *George Wakeman,*[6] b. Sept. 19, 1786, in Boylstown, N. Y. 2. *Jasper.* 3. *Samuel.* 4. *David.* 5. *Isaac.* 6. *William.* 7. *Mary.* 8. *Sarah.* (Order of births may not be correct.)
iii. JASPER.
iv. MARY.
v. A DAUGHTER, m. Lewis Joy of Guilford, Vt.

vi. DAVID, b. Feb. 22, 1767; m. Mercy Smalley; resided in Guilford and Rockingham, Vt. Children: 1. *Olive*,[6] b. May 26, 1790. 2. *David*, b. Feb. 14, 1792; d. Jan. 11, 1866; m. (1) July 2, 1812, Sophia Moore, b. July 6, 1792, d. Oct. 8, 1842; m. (2) Feb. 1, 1843, Eliza, b. Randolph, Vt., Nov. 24, 1807, d. Aug. 24, 1885, dau. of Roger and Elizabeth (Goodnough) Granger; resided in Randolph, Vt.; eleven children (eight by first wife). 3. *Philena*, b. June 7, 1794. 4. *Zoniah*, b. Sept. 4, 1796. 5. *Clarissa*, b. Aug. 19, 1799. 6. *Arial*, b. May 5, 1803; d. Oct. 22, 1845. 7. *Electa*, b. Apr. 17, 1805. 8. *Jasper*, b. Dec. 10, 1807. 9. *Mary*, b. Aug. 19, 1810; d. Aug. 20, 1848.

Children by second wife :

vii. LEONARD.
viii. SILAS.
ix. WILLIAM.
x. SAMUEL.

27. SILAS[4] PARTRIDGE (*Jonathan*,[3] *John*,[2] *John*[1]) was born in Medway, July 27, 1737. He married Abigail ———. They resided for a time at Peru, Mass.

Child :

i. MELETIAH,[5] b. Aug. 28, 1765.

28. THADDEUS[4] PARTRIDGE (*Jonathan*,[3] *John*,[2] *John*[1]) was born in Medway, Nov. 28, 1739. He married first, Dec. 8, 1763, Keziah Harding of Medway ; and married second, Sept. 8, 1766, Thankful, born in Medway, June 4, 1748, daughter of Eleazer and Bathsheba (Barber) Adams. They resided in Barre, Mass., where their children were born. He died there in 1827. She died Jan. 6, 1830.

Children by second wife :

JOHN,[5] b. Dec. 30, 1767; d. June 2, 1836; m. Hannah, b. Apr. 20, 1778, d. Sept. 22, 1850, dau. of Jonas and Thankful (Nourse) Rice. They resided in Barre. Children: 1. *Jonas Rice*,[6] b. Nov. 1, 1798; d. Oct. 20, 1869; m. Jan. 2, 1826, Prudence H., dau. of John Winn of West Boylston; removed in 1831 to Jo Daviess Co., Ill.; children. 2. *Alvin Adams*, b. Feb. 1, 1801; d. Sept. 18, 1870, unmarried. 3. *Thomas Jefferson*, b. Apr. 27, 1803; d. Feb. 15, 1855; m. Nov. 1830, Clara P., b. June 28, 1809, dau. of Roland Parkhurst of Hubbardston; removed to Whitside Co., Ill., in 1838; two children. 4. *Sarah Nourse*, b. May 27, 1805; d. July 9, 1866; m. Dec. 1841, John Wilder, b. Oct. 13, 1812, d. Jan. 28, 1887, son of Charles F. and Huldah (Wilder) Ross, of Wendell; resided in Wendell; several children. 5. *Mary Hall*, b. May 4, 1807; d. May 8, 1871, unmarried. 6. *James Madison*, b. Aug. 30, 1809; d. Aug. 10, 1884; m. Mch., 1837, Louisa, b. Dec. 15, 1814, d. Apr. 28, 1889, dau. of Lucius and Mary (Woodis) Spooner, of Oakham; resided in Worcester; five children. 7. *Eliza Phipps*, b. Dec. 5, 1811; d. June 12, 1847, unmarried. 8. *Charlotte*, b. Oct. 27, 1814; d. Apr. 11, 1891; m. Oct. 27, 1837, John Page, b. Mch. 9, 1806, d. Dec. 4, 1884, son of Aaron and Mary Butterfield, of Hardwick; resided in Oakham; children. 9. *Jane Rice*, b. Dec. 31, 1816; d. May 18, 1863; m. Dec. 24, 1837, Amory, b. Aug. 29, 1815, d. Dec. 20, 1884, son of Abel and Betsey (Hunt) Rice, of Marlboro'; resided in Lake Mills, Wis.; children. 10. *John Franklin*, b. Nov. 10, 1820; m. Nov. 14, 1853, Anna M. E., b. May 12, 1839, dau. of John William and Mary Eliza (Allen) Barton, of Shrewsbury; removed in 1860 to Owego, N. Y., where he has since resided; ten children.

ii. JONATHAN, b. Feb. 12, 1770; d. Apr. 9, 1770.
iii. ELEAZER, b. June 24, 1771; d. Feb. 15, 1850; m. Abigail Johnson. They resided in Barre, where his children were born. They were :

1. *William,*[6] b. Mch. 1, 1801; d. Mch. 1, 1862; m. Betsey, b. May 10, 1804, d. Mch. 5, 1871, dau. of Nathaniel and Esther (Johnson) Powers; removed to Wisconsin, about 1827; five children. 2. *Nancy,* b. Dec. 9, 1808; d. Mch. 22, 1875, unmarried. 3. *Ezra,* b. Feb. 1812; d. Apr. 1880, in Worcester, where he resided; m. Evelyn Howe, who d. June 1881; no children. 4. *George A.,* b. Nov. 22, 1814; d. Aug. 9, 1886; m. June 26, 1850, Caroline, b. Wilmington, Vt., May 10, 1823, d. May 19, 1883, dau. of Alpheus and Nancy (Conant) Simonds; resided in Worcester; no children. 5. *Micajah Reed,* b. Nov. 4, 1818; d. Apr. 30, 1887; m. May 3, 1850, Mary Jane, b. Berlin, Vt., Jan. 7, 1822, dau. of David B. and Lucy (Barker) Howe; resided in Worcester; no children.

iv. THANKFUL, b. Mch. 21, 1774; m. (1) Forbes, son of William and Anna (Forbes) Oliver, of Barre. One child. She m. (2) Amos Herrick. No children. She resided in Barre.

v. KEZIAH, b. May 12, 1776; d. Sept. 10, 1841; m. Apr. 4, 1798, Capt. Isaac Dennis, b. Jan. 26, 1775, d. Sept. 26, 1855. They resided in Barre. Children.

vi. PATTY, b. Feb. 19, 1779; d. Oct. 24, 1853; m. Nov. 8, 1804, Edmund Bangs of Barre.

vii. ANNA, b. Sept. 15, 1781; d. Aug. 7, 1851; m. Dec. 25, 1802, Rufus Holden, b. Mch. 28, 1774, d. Feb. 3, 1842. They resided in Barre. Six children.

viii. THADDEUS, b. Apr. 6, 1784; d. Feb. 8, 1851; m. Dorothy Woodis of Oakham, where they resided. No children.

ix. POLLY, b. Apr. 11, 1788; d. Sept. 19, 1798.

x. ARATHUSA, b. June 25, 1790; d. Apr. 13, 1875; m. May 30, 1820, Thomas Harlow, b. Aug. 9, 1772, d. Oct. 9, 1846. They resided in Barre. Two children.

29. REUBEN[4] PARTRIDGE (*Jonathan,*[3] *John,*[2] *John*[1]) was born in Medway, Nov. 21, 1741. He married, Feb. 6, 1766, Mary, born in Sherborn, Apr. 2, 1745, daughter of Moses and Deborah (Ivery) Perry. They resided in Sherborn until 1789, when they removed to Gardner, where they resided thereafter (Herrick's Hist. of Gardner). All but the youngest of their children were born in Sherborn. He died Aug. 21, 1801, and his son John was appointed administrator on his estate, Oct. 20, 1801 (Worcester Co. Prob., Case 45587).

Children:

i. MARY,[5] b. May 15, 1767; d. Mch. 29, 1801; m. May 15, 1791, Samuel Hill of Gardner; resided in Gardner. Two children.

ii. AMOS, b. Nov. 25, 1768; d. Sept. 9, 1854; removed to Augusta, Me., about 1801, where he resided; m. Hannah, b. Oxford, Mass., Mch. 21, 1770, d. Nov. 5, 1853, dau. of John and Hannah (Frost) Rockwood. Children: 1. *Anna,*[6] b. Oct. 31, 1794; d. Apr. 9, 1799. 2. *Hannah,* b. Jan. 2, 1798; d. Nov. 11, 1877. 3. *Amos Coolidge,* b. Aug. 15, 1799; d. July 11, 1872. 4. *Reuben,* b. July 24, 1801; d. Sept. 6, 1850. 5. *Nathaniel,* b. Aug. 12, 1803; d. Mch. 12, 1841. 6. *Joseph Rockwood,* b. June 19, 1805; d. Apr. 4, 1892. 7. *L'Orient,* b. Aug. 9, 1807; d. July 20, 1809. 8. *Joshua,* b. July 30, 1809; d. Feb. 28, 1823. 9. *Anna,* b. July 30, 1809; d. Jan. 20, 1833.

iii. ANNA, b. May 23, 1770; d. Sept. 21, 1789.

iv. DEBORAH, b. Apr. 25, 1773; m. Kendall, son of David and Rebecca (Belknap) Nichols, of Gardner; resided in Gardner. Children.

v. ELIZABETH, b. May 8, 1774; d. Sept. 22, 1776.

vi. MOSES, b. Mch. 8, 1776; d. June 28, 1849, in Augusta, Me., whither he removed about 1801; m. Ruth, b. Oxford, Mass., Mch. 27, 1777, dau. of John and Hannah (Frost) Rockwood. Several children.

vii. JOHN, b. Dec. 8, 1777; d. Jan. 15, 1831.

viii. NATHANIEL, b. Nov. 5, 1781; d. Nov. 14, 1793.

ix. WILLIAM, b. May 14, 1783; d. June 2, 1783.

x. WILLIAM, b. Mch. 16, 1788; d. June 30, 1836.

xi. ANNA, b. Dec. 2, 1789; d. Apr. 7, 1790.

30. JOHN[4] PARTRIDGE (*Jonathan,*[3] *John,*[2] *John*[1]) was born in Sherborn, Oct. 28, 1746. He married at Barre, Oct. 7, 1773, Mrs. Phebe Boyden, widow of Micah Boyden and daughter of Silas and Deborah (Buck) Sears, of Greenwich, Mass. They resided at Barre, where the births of four children are recorded. They may have removed from there after 1782.

Children:

  i.   SILAS,[5] b. June 5, 1774.
  ii. RHODA, b. July 10, 1776; m. May 7, 1806, James Newcomb of Oakham.
  iii. CHLOE, b. Sept. 20, 1779.
  iv. JOHN, b. Mch. 27, 1782.

31. JABEZ[4] PARTRIDGE (*Jonathan,*[3] *John,*[2] *John*[1]) was born in Sherborn, Dec. 11, 1748. He married, May 19, 1772, Anna, born in Sherborn, May 24, 1751, daughter of Jonathan and Deborah (Bullard) Twitchell. They resided at Sherborn until about 1780, when they removed to Gardner, where they afterwards lived.

Children:

  i.   ADAM,[5] b. Jan. 2, 1773; d. in infancy.
  ii. DEBORAH, b. Apr. 25, 1775; d. Oct. 22, 1846; m. Oct. 12, 1797, Elisha Pierce, who d. Apr. 1, 1858; resided in Westminster. Six children.
  iii. ADAM, b. Mch. 11, 1778; d. May 22, 1855; m. Mary, b. Nov. 12, 1781, d. Mch. 22, 1869, dau. of Oliver and Mary (Pierce) Jackson, of Westminster; resided in Gardner. Children: 1. *Asa,*[6] b. Aug. 1, 1800; d. May 28, 1883; m. Anne Williams; resided in Gardner; no children. 2. *Seneca,* b. July 26, 1802; d. Aug. 4, 1879; m. (1) Nov. 15, 1827, Sarah, b. Gardner, Sept. 16, 1805, d. Oct. 21, 1842, dau. of Jonathan and Beulah (Jackson) Brown; m. (2) June 9, 1844, Sarah, b. Jaffrey, N. H., Sept. 12, 1815, d. Feb. 23, 1887, dau. of Jeremy and Sarah (Gage) Underwood; resided in Gardner; seven children, four by first wife. 3. *Oran,* b. June 30, 1806; d. Nov. 2, 1893; m. Fitchburg, Sept. 15, 1835, Mary B., b. Gardner, Nov. 4, 1809, d. Jan, 2, 1888, dau. of Jonathan and Betsey (Bancroft) Wood; resided in Fitchburg; four children. 4. *Caroline,* b. Nov. 13, 1809; d. Mch. 15, 1900; m. Apr. 15, 1830, Isaac P., b. Gardner, Sept. 6, 1801, d. Dec. 11, 1833, son of Martin and Prudence Kendall; resided in Templeton, Mass., Jamaica, Vt., and Gardner, Mass.; five children. 5. *Loenza,* b. June 27, 1814; d. Apr. 25, 1875; m. Nathan Henry. 6. *Adam,* b. June 14, 1817; m. Dec. 25, 1848, Melissa. b. Jaffrey, N. H., Dec. 3, 1817, dau. of Jeremy and Sarah (Gage) Underwood; resided in New York City; two daughters. 7. *Mary,* b. Dec. 12, 1819; d. Dec. 29, 1876; m. Apr. 16, 1839, James C., b. Athol, July 10, 1817, son of Samuel and Lydia (Clements) Stearns; resided in Gardner and Millers Falls, Mass., and in 1855 settled in Hanno (now Sublette), Ills.; two children. 8. *Louisa,* b. May 3, 1822; m. Horatio Benton.
  iv. HANNAH, b. Dec. 7, 1780; m. John Bigelow; resided in Sherborn.
  v.   ANNA, b. Nov. 4, 1783; d. in Gardner, June 24, 1861; m. Rufus Whitcomb, of Gardner; removed to Canada. No children.
  vi. CYNTHIA, b. Dec. 1, 1785; d. July 1, 1860; m. Luke Whitney, b. Winchester, May 21, 1783, d. Gardner, Sept. 1, 1838; resided in Gardner. Eleven children.
  vii. MIRIAM, b. Aug. 20, 1787; m. David, b. Gardner, Apr. 10, 1786, son of Allen and Juda (Chase) Perley; resided in Gardner. Eleven children.
  viii. HENRY, b. June 5, 1791; d. Apr. 19, 1859; m. Anna Babcock; resided in Sherborn and Medfield. Children: 1. *Anna,*[6] m. —— Bigelow. 2. *Henry,* m. —— Leland. 3. *Caroline,* m. —— Stevens.

32. LOVET[4] PARTRIDGE (*Jonathan,*[3] *John,*[2] *John*[1]) was born in Sherborn, Sept. 13, 1750. He married in Mendon, May 19, 1774, Sarah Hayward of Mendon. They resided for a time in Uxbridge, where two children were born. Nothing is learned of them later than 1776.

Children:

i. ABIGAIL,[5] b. Feb. 24, 1775.
ii. DOLLY, b. Dec. 4, 1776.

33. STEPHEN[4] PARTRIDGE (*Jonathan,*[3] *John,*[2] *John*[1]) was born in Sherborn, Aug. 2, 1752. He married in Mendon, Jan. 4, 1776, Jemima, born in Mendon, July 6, 1758, daughter of Seth and Anna Taft. They resided in Mendon, where he died before May 25, 1790. His widow married second, Aug. 26, 1792, Peter Brown of Mendon.

Children:

i. LYDIA,[5] b. Mch. 31, 1777; m. Apr. 21, 1801, Asel Fairbanks of Mendon.
ii. MARY, b. June 17, 1780; m. Oct. 29, 1800, Amasa Albee of Mendon.

34. AMARIAH[4] PARTRIDGE (*Jonathan,*[3] *John,*[2] *John*[1]) was born in Barre, May 21, 1756. He was in the Revolutionary service (Mass. Archives). He resided in Montague, Mass. He had but one child.

Child:

i. FANNY,[5] b. Nov. 1, 1787; d. Mch. 10, 1876; m. Dec. 11, 1815, Elijah, b. Dec. 23, 1779, d. Oct. 24, 1861, son of Greenwood and Susan (Hammond) Carpenter, of Swansey, N. H.; resided in Swansey. Six children.

35. JAMES[4] PARTRIDGE (*James,*[3] *John,*[2] *John*[1]) was born in Medway, Oct. 10, 1730. He married Abigail ————, who died Mch. 24, 1798, aged 65 years. He settled in Boylston, Mass., and died in West Boylston in 1821.

Children:

i. RHODA,[5] b. Dec. 9, 1760; never married.
ii. ASA, b. Dec. 20, 1761; no further record.
iii. OZIAS, b. June 18, 1763; m. Zipporah ————; resided in Boylston for a time, then probably removed away. Children: 1. *Ozias,*[6] m. Nancy Whitman of Ashburnham; had child, Catharine Cushing,[7] b. Aug. 25, 1808, at Boylston, and perhaps others. 2. *Salmon,* b. Aug. 26, 1792, in Boylston; d. in Holden, Sept. 7, 1827; m. Nov. 24, 1814, in Holden, Susanna, b. there Jan. 5, 1793, dau. of Artemas and Susanna (Perry) Dryden; four children, b. Holden.
iv. ASAHEL, b. Mch. 7, 1766; d. Nov. 1889; m. Dec. 11, 1798, in Boylston, Polly (Knight) Butterfield, b. Phillipston, 1771, d. in Holden, Mch. 25, 1844, dau. of Daniel Knight; resided in Boylston, where their children were born, and later removed to Holden. Children: 1. *Horace,*[6] b. July 21, 1799; d. Sept. 25, 1800. 2. *Horace,* b. Nov. Nov. 13, 1801; d. Sept. 30, 1862; m. Nov., 1828, Sarah Abigail, b. Stow, June 18, 1807, d. Mch. 9, 1888, dau. of Sylvanus and Sarah (Moore) Morse; resided in Holden until 1846, and after that in Worcester; seven children. 3. *Adeline,* b. 1803; d. Jan. 9, 1844; m. Nov. 4, 1827, in Holden, Jason Knowlton; resided in Holden; five children.
v. JAMES, b. Oct. 20, 1770; d. Apr. 20, 1863; m. (1) Feb. 4, 1796, Polly Maynard, b. 1776, d. Sept. 30, 1796; m. (2) Sept. 27, 1798, in Sterling, Ruth, b. Shrewsbury, July 12, 1770, d. Apr. 18, 1851, dau. of Simeon and Lucy (Temple) Keyes; resided in Boylston. Children: 1. *Levi,*[6] b. Sept. 25, 1796; d. Oct. 11, 1796. 2. *Simeon,*

b. July 6, 1799; d. Feb. 20, 1866; m. (1) Dec. 5, 1831, Mary, dau. of Asa and Sarah (Thurston) Keyes, of Sterling, who d. Apr. 18, 1836; m. (2) Nov. 30, 1837, Sarah G., b. Boylston, Feb. 16, 1811, d. Worcester, Aug., 1890, dau. of Ebenezer and Betty (Greenwood) Hartshorn; resided in Boylston and later in Worcester; six children. 3. *Polly*, b. Aug. 17, 1800; d. Jan. 26, 1813. 4. *Abigail*, b. Sept. 6, 1802; m. (pub. Nov. 20, 1825) William Dodds, b. Boylston, May 1, 1796, son of Thaddeus and Polly (Dodds) Chenery. 5. *James Henry*, b. Apr., 1808; d. Feb. 25, 1809. 6. *Lucy Ann*, b. Sept. 29, 1813; d. May 14, 1860; unmarried.

36. MALACHI[4] PARTRIDGE (*James*,[3] *John*,[2] *John*[1]) was born in Medway, Nov. 30, 1731. He was in the Colonial service in 1754 (Mass. Archives). He settled in Sturbridge, where three children were born, and later removed to Holland, Mass., where he and his wife Abigail were living in 1796, with their son Isaac (Hampton Co. Deeds, vol. xxxiv, p. 161). She died in Sturbridge, Apr. 29, 1808.

Children :

i. ABIGAIL,[5] b. Aug. 15, 1768.
ii. ISAAC, b. Nov. 26, 1770; settled in Holland, Mass.
iii. PRIAH, b. Dec. 3, 1774.

37. ELEAZER[4] PARTRIDGE (*James*,[3] *John*,[2] *John*[1]) was born in Medway, Apr. 19, 1740. He married, in 1764, Lois, born June 15, 1744, daughter of Benjamin and Mehetabel (Thompson) Rockwood. They resided in Franklin, Mass., where their children were born. He died Mch. 19, 1834; and she died Dec. 16, 1812.

Children :

i. ELIAS,[5] b. Feb. 7, 1766; d. Mch. 6, 1857; m. Dec. 31, 1794, Abigail Chase of Sutton, who was b. Mch. 21, 1770, and d. Sept. 22, 1838; settled in Paris, Me. Children: 1. *Elias Chase*,[6] b. Dec. 12, 1795; d. Oct. 22, 1798. 2. *Cynthia*, b. Nov. 12, 1797; m. Nicholas Chesley. 3. *Austin*, b. Oct. 6, 1799; m. Jan. 14, 1833, Sarah, dau. of Gideon Powers; resided in Paris, Me.; five daughters. 4. *Electa*, b. Mch. 28, 1801; m. Feb. 23, 1823, Samuel Morrell. 5. *Bradford Chase*, b. Jan. 20, 1803; d. Jan. 6, 1805. 6. *Milo*, b. Aug. 27, 1804; d. Sept. 10, 1804. 7. *Abigail*, b. Feb. 20, 1806; m. (1) Jonas Kendall; m. (2) Liberty Hall. 8. *Caroline*, b. Aug. 23, 1808; m. Cornelius Morton. 9. *Adeline*, b. Aug. 23, 1808. 10. *Lois*, b. Aug. 8, 1810. 11. *Mary R.*, b. July 27, 1812; m. Hannibal Smith.
ii. SILENCE, b. Aug. 29, 1767; d. Sept. 21, 1767.
iii. LOIS, b. Sept. 17, 1768; d. July 9, 1786.
iv. TRYPHENA, b. Oct. 27, 1770; d. Mch. 11, 1771.
v. ASA, b. Apr. 19, 1773; d. Apr. 26, 1858; m. Jan. 1, 1801, Polly Richardson of Franklin, who d. Dec. 5, 1848, aged 76; resided in Franklin. No children.
vi. JULIA, b. Sept. 3, 1775: d. Feb. 14, 1782.
vii. PHINEAS, b. Mch. 16, 1777; d. Dec. 14, 1845; m. (1) May 7, 1801, Abigail Allen, b. Oct. 7, 1777, d. May 24, 1819; m. (2) Nov. 1, 1819, Polly Wheeler, b. Sept. 27, 1790; d. Jan. 9, 1866; resided in Franklin. Children: 1. *Allen*,[6] b. Jan. 18, 1804; d. Feb. 13, 1882; m. (1) Sept. 1, 1830, Nancy, dau. of John Emerson of Auburn, N. H., who d. July 15, 1845; m. (2) June 1, 1847, Sarah, b. New Hampton, N. H., Dec. 31, 1809, d. Apr. 21, 1900, dau. of David and Nancy (Pearson) Hanaford; resided at Amoskeag and Derry, N. H.; one son. 2. *Abigail Harding*, b. Feb. 20, 1806; d. Nov. 22, 1848; m. June 1, 1844, Luther Metcalf, b. Milford, Aug. 4, 1809, son of Joel and Clara (Metcalf) Hunt; resided in West Medway; one dau. 3. *Elmira Diantha*, b. Mch. 21, 1816; m. June 1, 1841, Oratio S., b. Holliston, Apr. 23, 1814, d. Apr. 21, 1899, son

of William and Sarah (Wiswell) Claflin; resided in Alexandria, Va., and Philadelphia, Pa.; six children. 4. *Clarissa Prentiss*, b. May 2, 1819; d. Mch. 19, 1854; unmarried. 5. *Asa*, b. Aug. 7, 1820; m. Oct. 8, 1847, Abigail, b. West Medway, Aug. 29, 1820, d. Feb. 4, 1890, dau. of Amos and Patience (Adams) Shumway; resided in Philadelphia, Pa., and Moorstown, N. J.; three children. 6. *John Wheeler*, b. Jan. 5, 1822; d. Sept. 28, 1899; m. Oct. 30, 1845, Caroline, b. West Medway, July 6, 1824, d. Feb. 26, 1884, dau. of Joel and Clara (Metcalf) Hunt; resided in Philadelphia, Pa., Worcester, Fitchburg and Roxbury, Mass.; three children. 7. *Sarah Putnam*, b. Nov. 10, 1823; d. May 11, 1892; m. Sept. 15, 1852, Ainsworth Rand, b. Gilmanton, N. H., Sept. 12, 1825, son of Luke Ainsworth and Grata (Rand) Spofford; resided in Cincinnati, O., and Washington, D. C.; three children. 8. *Charlotte*, b. Apr. 19, 1826; m. Aug. 31, 1846, Simeon H., b. Medway, Aug. 4, 1824, son of Simeon and Nancy (Hartshorn) Fuller; resided in Philadelphia, Pa., and Cambridge, Mass. 9. *George Brown*, b. Feb. 10, 1828; d. Jan. 25, 1853. 10. *Charles A.*, b. Feb. 2, 1831; m. May 18, 1852, Mary G. Peck; resided in Cincinnati, O.; six children. 11. *Edwin F.*, b. June 10, 1833; d. Redlands, Cal., Apr. 2, 1897; m. Dec. 17, 1857, Henrietta, b. at Catawissa, Pa., dau. of Samuel and Lydia (Hughes) Hartman; resided in Philadelphia, Pa.; five children.

viii. MEHETABEL, b. May 24, 1779; d. June 27, 1779.
ix. KEZIAH, b. Sept. 10, 1780; d. Sept. 27, 1864.
x. ELEAZER, b. May 27, 1782; d. Mch. 9, 1850; m. (1) Mch. 30, 1806, Mary Fisher, of Franklin, who d. Dec. 16, 1812; m. (2) Aug. 4, 1825, Hannah Keith of Walpole, who d. June 3, 1856, aged 58; resided in Franklin. Children: 1. *Mary Clark*,[6] b. Jan. 10, 1810; m. Sept. 5, 1837, Rev. William Phipps. 2. *Lois Rockwood*. 3. *Sylvia Pond*, b. Dec. 22, 1816; m. Joseph Lovell of Medway. 4. *Julia Ann*, b. July 5, 1826. 5. *Eliza Jane*, b. Apr. 21, 1829. 6. *Harriet Keith*, b. Feb. 14, 1831.
xi. ITHAMAR, b. May 27, 1782; d. Apr. 7, 1807.
xii. HANNAH, b. May 5, 1784; d. Sept. 20, 1838; unmarried.
xiii. NATHAN, b. Aug. 1, 1786; d. July 21, 1825; m. Jan. 12, 1815, Sarah Bassett; resided in Franklin. Children: 1. *Juliette Richardson*,[6] b. Oct. 23, 1815. 2. *Elias Anson*, b. July 1, 1818. 3. *Mary Bassett*, b. Dec. 15, 1819. 4. *George Ithamar*, b. July 23, 1822. 5. *Harriet Maria*, b. Aug. 1, 1824; m. Oct. 31, 1844, James D. Miller.

38. STEPHEN[4] PARTRIDGE (*James*,[3] *John*,[2] *John*[1]) was born in Medway, July 10, 1746. He married in Uxbridge, February, 1772, Esther, born there June 14, 1751, daughter of Thomas and Abigail (Marsh) Emerson. They resided in Medway until 1775, when they removed to Shrewsbury, remaining there until 1779, when they migrated to Maine, in the Kennebec river region, a short time later removing to Rochester, Vt., and from there to Wilmington, Essex Co., N. Y., later going, in 1815, to Ohio, and settling near Columbus. He died in Amity, O., June 14, 1818; and she died in Marysville, O., Feb. 10, 1835. Two children were born in Medway, two in Shrewsbury, and the others in Rochester, Vt.

Children:

i. HANNAH[5], b. Jan. 30, 1773.
ii. JUDITH, b. Apr. 20, 1774: d. at Marysville, O.; unmarried.
iii. LEWIS, b. Aug. 26, 1776; d. Nov. 2, 1812; m. Phebe Austin; resided in Essex Co., N. Y. Children: 1. *Hiram*,[6] m. (1) Louisa Reynolds; m. (2) Eliza Hutchinson; ten children, four by first wife. 2. *Phebe*, m. Augustus Hudson; six children. 3. *Alvin*, d. young. 4. *Philena*, m. —— McLeod; six children. 5. *Lewis*, m. Adeline Reynolds; one child. 6. *Enoch*, m. Betsey Ray; children. 7. *Asenath*, m. David Sanborn; three children. 8. *Stillman*, d. young.

iv. LUCRETIA, b. Nov. 7, 1778.
v. STEPHEN, b. May 1, 1781; killed at the battle of Plattsburg, Sept. 5, 1814; m. Lois Wheeler. Children: 1. *Amanda,*[6] m. ——— Searl, of Clintonville, N. Y.; two children. 2. *Mason.* 3. *Daniel.* 4. *Martin.*
vi. ESTHER, b. Nov. 12, 1782; m. Oliver, b. May 26, 1781, in Woodstock, Vt., son of Stephen and Mary (Shaw) Delano; settled in Worthington, O., in 1815, where he d. Jan., 1820. Three sons.
vii. EUNICE, b. May 11, 1785; d. May 27, 1807.
viii. REUBEN, b. Sept. 12, 1788; d. Nov. 9, 1853; m. in 1810, Diadama Ray, b. Jan. 4, 1787, d. Oct. 17, 1861; resided in Wilmington, N.Y. Children: 1. *Persis,*[6] b. Mar. 31, 1811; Nov. 12, 1889; m. (1) in 1835, Joseph Shaw of Keene, N. Y., who d. in Rootstown, O., in 1838; m. (2) in 1841, Rev. Hiram Miner of Canton, O.; m. (3) in 1849, Seth Jennings of Freedom, O.; seven children, two by first, two by second, and three by third husband. 2. *Eunice,* b. July 13, 1813; d. May 2, 1850; m. Nov. 20, 1834, John Southmayd; six children. 3. *Stephen,* b. Sept. 21, 1815; d. Oct. 4, 1881; m. Harriet Knowles; resided in St. Louis, Mo.; two daughters. 4. *Caroline,* b. Nov. 4, 1817; d. Sept. 12, 1891; m. Sept. 12, 1839, Uriah D., b. Stukely, Quebec, May 7, 1818, d. Fond du Lac, Wis., June 3, 1898, son of Moses and Frances (Moffatt) Mihills; resided in Fond du Lac, Wis.; ten children. 5. *Prindle,* b. Jan. 4, 1820; m. Sept. 17, 1846, Lucinda, b. Claremont, N. H., Feb. 7, 1825, dau. of Seth and Olive (Ashley) Bunnell; resided in Reedsburg and Cazenovia, Wis., and St. Paul, Minn.; three children. 6. *Ermina,* b. Jan. 10, 1822; m. July 17, 1845, Willard Bell, b. Apr. 3, 1823, d. Jan. 25, 1887; resided in Keene, N. Y.; five children.
ix. ADRIAL, b. Nov. 4, 1790; m. ——— Stickney; resided in Salem, N. Y. Children: 1. *Moors.*[6] 2. *Cyrus.* 3. *Malinda.*
x. CYRUS, b. May 22, 1794; d. Oct. 22, 1836; m. Mrs. Lucinda (Carpenter) Lee, who was b. Sept. 15, 1794, d. Oct. 4, 1850; settled in Marysville, O., in 1833. Children: 1. *Worthy,*[6] b. Dec. 26, 1817; d. Nov. 15, 1857; m. Clementine Lewis; moved to Texas; five children. 2. *Orson Monroe,* b. 1820; d. July 14, 1822. 3. *Reuben L.,* b. Sept. 10, 1823; d. July 17, 1900; m. Oct. 20, 1846, Maria, b. Dec. 18, 1825, dau. of Adam and Katharine (Wolford) Wolford, of Marysville, O.; resided in Marysville; six children. 4. *John Wesley,* b. Oct. 3, 1829; d. July 12, 1867; m. Caroline Lewis; went to Texas; several children.

39. JOEL[4] PARTRIDGE (*James,*[3] *John,*[2] *John*[1]) was born in Medway, Feb. 19, 1748. He resided near Medway Village, on the farm owned by his father. He married Waitstill, born in West Medway, Mar. 6, 1755, died in Medway, Mar. 8, 1825, daughter of Ezekiel and Rebecca (Cozzins) Morse. He died Feb. 13, 1823. Their children were born in Medway.

Children:

i. EZEKIEL[5], b. July 1, 1775; d. Feb. 19, 1826; m. Feb. 27, 1800, in Medway, Deborah Harding, b. May 26, 1775; resided in Medway until 1808, when they removed to Worcester, where they afterwards lived. Children, four oldest b. in Medway, others in Worcester: 1. *Untimely,*[6] b. Oct. 2, 1800; d. Oct. 3, 1800. 2. *Elizabeth,* b. Oct. 8, 1802; d. Sept. 28, 1887; m. Sept. 24, 1823, in Worcester, Nathaniel H., b. Worcester, June 9, 1801, d. Dec. 16, 1891, son of John and Sarah (Healy) Stowe; settled, soon after marriage, at Ashville, N. Y., removing from there, in 1836, to Wattsburg, Erie Co., Penn., where they thereafter resided; eight children. 3. *Elbridge Gerry,* b. Oct. 21, 1804; resided in Worcester; several children. 4. *Almond,* b. Feb. 20, 1807; d. Aug. 4, 1838; m. May 4, 1830, Mehetabel, b. West Boylston, May 27, 1813, d. Jan. 19, 1899, dau. of Jonathan Lovell; removed in 1833 to Jamestown, N. Y., where they afterwards lived; three children. 5. *Joel,*

b. Nov. 11, 1808; d. May 22, 1896; m. (1) in Worcester, Feb. 26, 1831, Azuba, b. Worcester, Aug. 25, 1813, d. Jamestown, N. Y., Apr. 26, 1841, dau. of Paul and Azuba (Newton) Goodell; m. (2) in Jamestown, N. Y., Dec. 31, 1841, Mary R., b. Stratford, Vt., Dec. 22, 1815, d. Jamestown, N. Y., Dec. 2, 1888, dau. of Adonijah and Betsey (Bacon) Pennock; six children by first wife, and six by second wife, all b. in Jamestown, N. Y., where he resided. 6. *Abigail Harding*, b. Dec. 27, 1810; d. Apr. 26, 1898; m. Mar. 17, 1831, in Worcester, Israel Goodell Moore, b. Worcester, Jan. 2, 1809, d. Sept. 24, 1894; resided in West Boylston until 1837, removing thence to Oak Hill, near Jamestown, N. Y., where they afterwards lived; three children. 7. *Albert Adams*, b. May 2, 1814; d. Apr. 18, 1899; m. in Worcester, Apr. 17, 1837, Mary Adeline, b. Worcester, June 27, 1812, d. Feb. 25, 1895, dau. of Adolphus and Sarah E. Taftt; resided in Worcester until 1840, removing thence to Jamestown, N. Y., where they thereafter resided; nine children. 8. *James Seth Harding*, b. Oct. 19, 1819; m. (1) in Milford, Maria Antoinette, b. Hopkinton, in 1820, dau. of Leonard Walker; m. (2) ———; resided at Hopkinton, Mass., until 1879; now living in Jamestown, N. Y.; children.

ii. ABIGAIL, b. Jan. 9, 1777; d. in 1860; m. Ezra Adams.
iii. CATHARINE, b. Apr. 1, 1779; d. in 1871; m. Stephen Adams.
iv. TAMAR, b. Aug. 8, 1781; m. Job,[5] son of Job Partridge (45).
v. JOEL, b. Mar. 1, 1784; d. Aug. 19, 1852; inherited his father's homestead near Medway, where he resided; m. (1) Feb. 26, 1807, Sarah, b. in 1785, dau. of Stephen and Eunice (Clark) Clark, who d. July 19, 1820; m. (2) Nov. 16, 1820, Joanna Sanford, who d. Apr. 15, 1853. Children, four by first wife, and two by second wife: 1. *Remembrance*,[6] b. Apr. 18, 1808; d. May 1, 1808. 2. *Clark*, b. Apr. 1, 1809; d. Nov. 17, 1885; m. (1) Apr. 6, 1830. Mary, b. Medway, Mar. 17, 1811, d. Mar. 23, 1834, dau. of Seth and Mary (Learned) Harding; m. (2) Mrs. Abigail (Harding) Partridge, sister of his first wife and widow of William Partridge; resided in Medway; one child by first wife. 3. *Joel Gilbert*, b. May 22, 1813; d. Feb. 18, 1846; m. (1) Emeline Richardson, who d. Apr. 20, 1840; m. (2) Roxanna Richardson; resided in Medway; three children by first, and two by second wife. 4. *Sarah Ann*, b. Dec. 3, 1818; m. June 14, 1840, Joseph Bullard. 5. *Edmund James*, b. Apr. 6, 1827; d. May 31, 1828. 6. *Lydia Sanford*, b. Sept. 11, 1830; m. Apr. 12, 1853, Addison P. Thayer.
vi. JERUSHA, b. May 2, 1787; m. David Mann of Westborough, Mass.
vii. EDE, b. June 25, 1789; m. Nathaniel Clark.
viii. JAMES, b. Sept. 3, 1793; d. Apr. 26, 1816.

40. NATHAN[4] PARTRIDGE (*James*,[3] *John*,[2] *John*[1]) was born in Medway, Mar. 26, 1751. He married Meletiah, born in Bellingham, Feb. 28, 1755, daughter of Deacon Joseph Holbrook. Nathan Partridge died in Medway, May 25, 1785. His children were born there.
  Children: •

i. LOVINA, [5] b. Jan. 8, 1777; d. July 10, 1782.
ii. NATHAN, b. Dec. 27, 1778; d. Feb. 20, 1854; settled in Barre, Mass., where he m. Feb. 17, 1804, Isabella Fessenden, b. Jan. 16, 1780; their children were born in Barre. Children: 1. *Hiram F.*, b. June 16, 1805; m. May 5, 1830, in Barre, Mary Jenkins, b. Boston, in 1804; settled in Naples, N. Y., where he d. in 1844; four children. 2. *Lavinia E.*, b. May 9, 1808. 3. *Albert H.*, b. Jan. 19, 1811; m. (1) at Leonidas, Mich., Jan. 24, 1847, Versilda Pierce, b. at Naples, N. Y., in 1828, d. Leonidas, Mich., in 1848; m. (2) at Leonidas, May 26, 1850, Mrs. Cornelia B. (Noyes) Eggleston, b. Florence, O., in 1822; resided in Leonidas, Mich., where he died in 1894; one child by first, four by second wife. 4. *Augusta M.*, b. Aug. 28, 1815; d. in 1834. 5. *Winfield Scott*, b. June 13, 1817; d. Naples, N. Y., in 1849. 6. *William A.*, b. Sept. 10, 1819; m. at

Naples, N. Y., May 18, 1846, Lucetta A. Gates, b. in Barre, in 1817; resided in Barre, where he d. in 1875; four children.
iii. SUSANNA, b. Nov. 30, 1788; m. Capt. Asa Fiske of Holliston.

41. ELISHA[4] PARTRIDGE (*Eleazer,[3] Eleazer,[2] John[1]*) was born in Dedham (now Walpole), Mar. 16, 1716. He settled in Stoughton, Mass., where, on Mar. 1, 1738, he purchased 100 acres of land of Jedediah Morse (Suffolk Co. Deeds, Lib. lvii., p. 193). He married, Dec. 11, 1740, in Stoughton, Hannah Wellman of Norton. He was in the Colonial service, from Stoughton, in 1757 (Mass. Archives). The births of four children are recorded in Stoughton.
Children :
i. SARAH,[5] b. Oct. 25, 1741.
ii. RACHEL, b. Oct. 24, 1743.
iii. HANNAH, b. July 12, 1745.
iv. EZRA, b. Oct. 25, 1747.

42. HENRY[4] PARTRIDGE (*Eleazer,[3] Eleazer,[2] John[1]*) was born in Walpole, Sept. 6, 1724. He married, July 2, 1747, Mary, born in Dedham, Aug. 25, 1723, daughter of Moses and Mary (Clapp) Chamberlain. They resided in Walpole, where their children were born.
Children :
i. HENRY,[5] b. Feb. 17, 1748; m. Oct. 16, 1771, Frances, b. Walpole, Dec. 19, 1753, dau. of Jonathan and Frances Kendall. They resided in Walpole. Children: 1. *Mary,[6]* b. Mch. 1, 1773; m. Feb. 23, 1797, David Bruce, who d. in Walpole, May 12, 1835, aged 68; resided in Walpole; several children. 2. *Thankful,* b. Jan. 1, 1775; d. young. 3. *Frances (Fanny),* b. June 27, 1776; m. May 28, 1794, Sewall, b. Walpole, Jan. 16, 1768; son of Eliphalet and Hannah Clapp. 4. *Henry,* b. Feb. 16, 1779; m. Oct. 3, 1802, Catharine, b. Walpole, Dec. 28, 1780, dau. of Major Seth and Joanna Bullard. 5. *Nancy,* b. May 9, 1781; m. July 11, 1804, Daniels, b. Medfield, in 1777, son of Francis and Mary (Daniels) Hamant. She d. in 1815; and he m. (2) Patty Turner of Walpole. He d. in 1854. Three children by first wife. 6. *Eleazer,* b. Mch. 16, 1783. 7. *Jonathan Kendall,* b. Jan. 28, 1785. 8. *Patty,* b. Feb. 26, 1787; m. Nov. 24, 1805, Daniel Payson of Walpole. 9. *Curtis,* b. Apr. 28, 1789; m. Aug. 17, 1815, Mary Morey of Walpole. He d. soon after; and she m. (2) Dec. 9, 1819, Jonathan Newell of Walpole. 10. *Willard,* b. Jan. 17, 1792. 11. *Sukey,* b. Feb. 17, 1794. 12. *Thankful,* b. Nov. 29, 1795.
ii. MARY, b. Aug. 17, 1750; d. Oct. 21, 1756.
iii. THANKFUL, b. Oct. 11, 1752; d. Sept. 29, 1756.
iv. ELEAZER, b. Aug. 24, 1755; d. Oct. 13, 1776.
v. EZEKIEL, b. Apr. 27, 1758; d. Sept. 19, 1776.
vi. RUTH, b. May 3, 1760; d. Sept. 30, 1776.
vii. OTIS, b. Feb. 16, 1764; m. Nov. 16, 1785, Hannah, b. Walpole, Nov. 1, 1767, dau. of Samuel and Anna (Hartshorn) Smith. They resided in Walpole until about 1810, when they removed to Templeton, Mass., where they afterwards lived. He d. Nov. 23, 1827. Children: 1. *Ezekiel,[6]* b. Oct. 28, 1786; d, Apr. 2, 1869; m. Mch. 31, 1808, Anna, b. Walpole, May 1, 1787, d. July 2, 1873, dau. of Palmer Morey. They resided in Walpole until 1810 or 1811, removing thence to Templeton, where they afterwards lived. Twelve children. 2. *Ruth,* b. Aug. 27, 1788; d. Mch. 22, 1864; m. in Walpole, May 31, 1808, Joel Fales, b. Aug. 31, 1782, d. Oct. 30, 1866. They resided in Templeton. Thirteen children. 3. *Otis,* b. Mch. 8, 1790; d. Nov. 1, 1853; m. Jan. 7, 1813, Unity, b. June 4, 1793, d. Dec. 27, 1869, dau. of Abiather and Sarah Fales. They resided in Templeton. Ten children. 4. *Herman,* b. Aug. 25, 1791; d. Oct. 17, 1875; m. (1) Mch. 2, 1817, Harriet Allen; m. (2) Apr.

10, 1829, Betsey Jones, who d. Oct. 11, 1869. Three children by first wife. *5. Hervey,* b. Aug. 25, 1791; d. Mch. 28, 1859; m. in Walpole, Nov. 6, 1814, Rachel Paine, b. Foxboro', Aug. 9, 1789, d. Aug. 30, 1856. They resided in Walpole and Warwick, Mass. Seven children. *6. Hannah,* b. Oct. 25, 1793; d. Nov. 16, 1865; m. (1) May 25, 1824, Uriah Merritt, who d. in a few years; m. (2) Dec. 18, 1829, Aaron Jones of Templeton, b. July 30, 1790, d. Sept. 12, 1858. They resided in Templeton. Two children by first husband; five by second husband. *7. Grata,* b. July 10, 1795; d. Feb. 3, 1869; m. Mch. 3, 1815, Jonas Rice, b. July 15, 1791, d. Mch. 20, 1862. They resided in Templeton. Ten children. *8. Warren,* b. Jan. 16, 1797; d. Dec. 24, 1852; m. Dec. 4, 1831, Amorette Potter, b. Oct. 2, 1807, d. Apr. 12, 1888. They resided in Princeton, Mass. Six children. *9. Emmons,* b. Jan. 8, 1799; d. Aug. 8, 1873; m. Feb. 5, 1823, Charlotte, b. Wrentham, Oct. 24, 1802, dau. of Adam and Hannah (Clapp) Boyden. Four children. 10. *Harriet,* b. Jan. 20, 1801; d. July 5, 1836; m. Dec. 2, 1819, Luther Baker, b. Jan. 12, 1797, d. Feb. 4, 1874. Five children. 11. *Lucy,* b. Jan. 13, 1803; d. Oct. 15, 1842; m. Nov., 1823, Abel Davis, b. Feb. 16, 1794, d. Feb. 10, 1858. Nine children. 12. *Mary,* b. Sept. 18, 1804; d. June 4, 1875; m. Jan. 27, 1831, Augustus Appleton Jones, b. Jan. 4, 1797. They resided in Templeton. Five children. 13. *Maynard,* b. Mch. 16, 1807; d. Sept. 22, 1884; m. Apr. 13, 1831, Mary H. Upham, b. Templeton, Feb. 21, 1810, d. May 15, 1882. They resided in Templeton and Phillipston. Three children. 14. *Julia,* b. April 2, 1809; d. Sept. 12, 1830, unmarried. 15. *Amanda,* b. July 13, 1811; d. Aug. 26, 1881; m. May 1, 1831, Uriah B. Moore, who d. Sept. 22, 1884. Eight children. 16. *Samuel Smith,* b. Apr. 18, 1813; d. Jan. 20, 1872; m. (1) Aug. 18, 1835, Susan J. Seekel, who d. June 30, 1845; m. (2) Nov. 12, 1846, Lucy A. Gifford, who d. Dec. 26, 1895, aged 80 yrs. Two children by first wife; six by second wife.

43. LEVI[4] PARTRIDGE (*Job,*[3] *Eleazer,*[2] *John*[1]) was born in Wrentham, Sept. 22, 1739. He married, in 1766, Lydia Miller of Keene, N. H. She was born Oct. 25, 1747, and died Nov. 28, 1798. He first settled in Dublin, N. H., but removed about 1779 to Keene. Soon after 1800 he located at Stockbridge, Vt., where he afterwards lived; and where he died Jan. 29, 1813.

Children:

i. LEVI,[5] b. Apr. 28, 1768; d. in infancy.
ii. LYDIA, b. July 30, 1769; d. in 1842. Nothing further known.
iii. LEVI, b. Mch. 13, 1771; d. Mch. 18, 1860; settled in Glover, Vt.; had three sons and three daughters, names unknown.
iv. RHODA, b. Oct. 13, 1774; d. July 6, 1862. Nothing further known.
v. ANNA, b, July 10, 1778; d. Nov. 30, 1858. Nothing further known.
vi. MARTHA, b. Aug. 17, 1780; d. Oct. 24, 1862. Nothing further known.
vii. EXPERIENCE (PEDEE), b. July 27, 1782; d. Apr. 15, 1835. Nothing further known.
viii. ASA, b. Apr. 18, 1786; d. Oct. 26, 1851; m. June, 1808, in Westmoreland, N. H., Charlotte, b. Milford, N. H., Aug. 19, 1786, dau. of David and Lydia (Twitchell) French. She d. July 5, 1871. They resided in Royalton and Stockbridge, Vt. Children: 1. *Caroline,*[6] b. Sept. 27, 1811; d. May 2, 1860; m. Dec. 10, 1840, in Stockbridge, Samuel A., b. Moriah, N. Y., July 18, 1813, d. Northfield, Vt., June 3, 1861, son of Moody and Betsey (Abbott) Johnson. They resided in Stockbridge and Northfield, Vt. Two children. 2. *Hiram Cheney,* b. July 5, 1814; d. Mch. 17, 1815. 3. *Almira,* b. Mch. 20, 1816; d. July 24, 1872; m. in Stockbridge, Vt., Jan. 14, 1834, Warren, b. Stockbridge, Jan. 17, 1797, d. Nov. 24, 1861, son of Uriah and Persis (Goodnow) Hayden. They resided in Stockbridge and Granville, Vt. One son. 4. *Louisa,* b. June

22, 1818; d. Apr. 8, 1893; m. May 6, 1839, Jonas, b. Granville, Vt., Nov. 19, 1812, d. in Rochester, Vt., Nov. 8, 1892, son of Joel and Persis Rice. They resided in Granville, Stockbridge and Rochester, Vt. Six children. 5. *Asa Cheney*, b. July 9, 1820; d. Nov. 2, 1893; m. in Wheeling, W. Va., Oct. 17, 1852, Elizabeth Ann, b. Andover, N. H., June 24, 1824, d. June 8, 1881, dau. of Joseph and Nancy B. (Runnels) Philbrick. They settled in Wheeling, W. Va., in 1848, removing in 1864 to Boston. In 1877 they located in Oakland, Cal., and four years later in San Francisco, where they afterwards lived. Nine children. 6. *Hiram French*, b. May 14, 1823; d. June 14, 1894. 7. *Pedee Alvira*, b. July 14, 1825; m. (1) in Sharon, Vt., Dec. 17, 1825, Rev. John C., b. Fairlee, Vt., Dec. 28, 1807, d. Dec. 9, 1865, son of John Baldwin; m. (2) Sept., 1875, James A., b. Middlebury, Vt., Dec. 14, 1814, d. Aug. 24, 1894, son of Moses and Keziah Severance. They resided in East Middlebury, Vt. No children. 8. *Charles Franklin*, b. Mch. 9, 1828; m. Dec. 18, 1855, Sarah A., b. Stockbridge, Vt., Feb. 7, 1835, dau. of Luther and Lucy (Rogers) Rice. They resided in East Middlebury, Vt. Five children.

ix. ZIBA, b. July 28, 1788; m. Dec. 7, 1812, Mehitabel Gale, b. Dec. 30, 1789, d. Sept. 22, 1826. They resided in Glover, Vt. After death of his wife he removed West, place unknown. No further record. Children: 1. *Merrill.*[6] 2. *Lucius.* 3. *Olin*, b. Dec. 17, 1816; m. Jan. 16, 1853, Julia A. B., b. Sept. 25, 1827, in Bradford, Vt., dau. of Abraham and Mary (Jenkins) Shaw. They resided in Ripon, Wis., where he d. Aug. 16, 1861. One son.

44. BENJAMIN[4] PARTRIDGE (*Benjamin,*[3] *Eleazer,*[2] *John*[1]) was born in Bellingham, Oct. 24, 1739. He married in Bellingham, Oct. 21, 1765, Mary, born there Apr. 27, 1743, daughter of Oliver and Elizabeth (Smith) Perry. He was in the Revolutionary service (Mass. Archives), and died at Ticonderoga, N. Y., Sept. 16, 1776. Distribution of his personal property was made among his widow and children, Simeon (eldest son), Jairus, Mary, Sabria and Lois, Sept. 5, 1777 (Suffolk Co. Prob. Rec., vol. lxxvi, p. 185). His widow married second, Apr. 26, 1780, John, son of John and Mary Coombs of Bellingham. Benjamin[4] resided in Bellingham, where his children were born.

Children :

i. SIMEON,[5] was living in 1777. No further record.
ii. JAIRUS, b. June 15, 1768; m. in Holden, Apr. 7, 1791, Betty, b. there Mch. 6, 1772, dau. of Paul and Eunice (Lovell) Goodale. They resided in Winchendon for a time, where he d. before July 1, 1823 (Worcester Co. Prob., case 45553). Child: 1. *Naomi,*[6] who was living in Winchendon in 1823. Perhaps other children.
iii. MARY, b. Apr. 10, 1772; d. Oct. 6, 1795; m. Apr. 3, 1791, Nathan, b. Bellingham, Nov. 28, 1756, son of Daniel and Deborah (Harding) Penniman. They resided in Bellingham. Two children.
iv. SABRIA, b. Mch. 13, 1775; m. (1) Dec. 13, 1792, Calvin, b. Jan. 6, 1765, d. Aug. 8, 1825, son of Ebenezer and Abigail (Adams) Holbrook. They resided in Mendon and Milford. Ten children. She m. (2) Apr. 5, 1827, Simeon, b. June 23, 1760, d. in 1848, son of John and Sarah Albee of Milford. They resided in Milford. She d. in 1852.
v. LOIS, b. Apr. 14, 1777; d. Oct. 12, 1795.

45. JOB[4] PARTRIDGE (*Benjamin,*[3] *Eleazer,*[2] *John*[1]) was born in Bellingham, Feb. 28, 1742. He married, Nov, 29, 1769, Deborah, born in Medway, June 2, 1747, daughter of Jonas and Experience (Leland) Fairbanks. They resided in Bellingham, where their children were born. He died Sept. 10, 1823; and she died Nov. 14, 1827.

Children:

i. ELIZABETH,⁵ b. July 18, 1770; d. July 18, 1770.
ii. HANNAH, b. July 18, 1770; d. July 18, 1770.
iii. SARAH, b. Aug. 22, 1771; d. Aug. 11, 1825; m. Jan. 21, 1798, Ichabod, b. Wrentham, Feb. 22, 1762, d. in Franklin, Aug. 26, 1826, son of Benjamin and Lois (Partridge) Pond. They resided in Franklin. Two children.
iv. AARON, b. Sept. 24, 1773; d. March 7, 1846; m. Apr. 11, 1799, Abigail, b. Wrentham, Mch. 7, 1778, dau. of Hezekiah and Lois (Metcalf) Pond. They resided in Bellingham until about 1812, when they removed to Milford. All their children were born in Bellingham. Children: 1. *Nancy,*⁶ b. June 24, 1800; d. Aug., 1872; m. Apr. 23, 1823, Theron, b. Milford, Mch. 29, 1798, son of Calvin and Sabria (Partridge) Holbrook. They resided in Milford. Six children. 2. *Abigail,* b. Apr. 3, 1802; d. Dec. 28, 1868; m. Dec. 3, 1818, Abel, b. Milford, Mch. 24, 1797, d. Dec. 25, 1872, son of Abel and Anna (Wood) Albee. They resided in Milford. Five children. 3. *Lucinda,* b. Apr. 5, 1804; m. Oct. 24, 1827, Abijah Stearns Clark. 4. *Aaron,* b. May 2, 1806; d. in Upton, Sept. 7, 1879; m. in Shelburne, May 25, 1828, Hannah Fisk, b. Shelburne, Dec. 8, 1802. They resided in Framingham and Upton. Five children. 5. *Rhoda,* b. June 19, 1809; m. Mch. 4, 1845, Samuel Kinsman. 6. *Elmira,* b. Apr. 21, 1811; m. Mch. 12, 1848, Cyrus Hill of Medway.
v. DEBORAH, b. July 15, 1775; d. Mch. 20, 1815; m. int. pub. July 17, 1803, to Timothy Ellis of Franklin. They resided in Franklin. Six children.
vi. BENJAMIN, b. Apr. 6, 1777; d. Mch. 14, 1853; m. Jan. 16, 1798, Milcah, b. Franklin, July 28, 1778, d. Apr. 5, 1858, dau. of Benjamin and Lois (Partridge) Pond. They resided in Bellingham until 1800, removing thence to Charlton, where they thereafter lived. Children: 1. *Sylvia,*⁶ b. Mch. 3, 1799; d. Mch. 3, 1898; m. Mch. 24, 1822, Ebenezer, b. Charlton, Sept. 4, 1798, d. June 23, 1853, son of Ebenezer and Lydia (Davis) White. They resided in Charlton. Children. 2. *Benjamin,* b. in 1802; d. Jan. 16, 1857; m. Harriet, dau. of William and Sabra (Stevens) Needham. They resided in Charlton. Three children. 3. *Mary,* b. in 1804; d. Nov., 1873; m. John Morey of Charlton. They resided in Charlton. Children. 4. *Leonard Pond,* b. Apr. 21, 1810; d. Jan. 7, 1859; m. Oct. 12, 1838, Sophronia N., b. Charlton, Apr. 20, 1819, dau. of Timothy and Sophia (Merriam) Morse. They resided in Charlton. Four children. 5. *Elijah Fairbanks,* b. Dec. 31, 1812; m. Apr. 18, 1838, Ruth S., b. Charlton, Nov. 17, 1818, dau. of David and Ruth (Alexander) Morse. They resided in Charlton. Three children.
vii. JOB, b. May 21, 1779; d. May 24, 1826; m. Apr. 12, 1804, Tamar, b. Aug. 8, 1781, d. Jan. 19, 1831, dau. of Joel (39) and Waitstill (Morse) Partridge. They resided in Bellingham and Milford. Children: 1. *Horace,*⁶ b. Apr. 23, 1805; d. Sept. 2, 1853; m. ———. One dau. 2. *Mary,* b. Jan. 18, 1807; m. ——— Adams; resided in West Medway. Children. 3. *Edson,* b. Jan. 6, 1809; d. Apr. 24, 1836. 4. *Joanna,* b. Sept. 12, 1811; d. June 1, 1823. 5. *Joseph,* b. Aug. 24, 1814; d. in 1896; resided in Holliston. Several children. 6. *Betsey,* b. June 6, 1816; d. Mch. 14, 1854. 7. *Eda,* b. Oct. 16, 1818; d. June 14, 1854. 8. *David Sanford,* b. Oct. 4, 1820; m. ———. Children. 9. *George Job,* b. May 19, 1826; d. July 26, 1897; m. Hannah B., b. Holliston, June 8, 1825, d. June 28, 1901, dau. of Jonas Curtis. They resided in Holliston. One son.
viii. RHODA, b. Aug. 11, 1781; m. in Milford, May 19, 1805, Ephraim, b. Milford, Oct. 17, 1781, son of Isaac and Elizabeth Littlefield. They resided in Petersham.
ix. BATHSHEBA, b. Dec. 5, 1784; d. Feb. 22, 1824, unmarried.
x. EXPERIENCE, b. Sept. 14, 1786; d. Oct. 8, 1841; m. Dec. 2, 1806, Ellery, b. Franklin, Mch. 10, 1783, d. in Medway, Jan. 8, 1871, son of John and Abigail (Partridge) Allen. They resided in Franklin. Nine children.

xi. MOSES, b. Sept., 1788; d. Sept. 26, 1824; studied theology under Rev. Nathaniel Emmons of Franklin, and was ordained to the ministry; m. not long before his death. No children.

xii. JONAS, b. April 27, 1790; d. May 8, 1790.

46. JOSEPH[4] PARTRIDGE (*Benjamin,*[3] *Eleazer,*[2] *John*[1]) was born in Bellingham, July 24, 1747. He married, April 13, 1775, Catharine, born in Medway, Apr. 9, 1753, died July 13, 1828, daughter of Benjamin and Elizabeth Richardson. They resided in Bellingham, where their children were born. He died May 24, 1810.

Children:

i. LIBERTY,[5] b. Jan. 13, 1776; d. Aug. 24, 1867; m. (1) Jan. 15, 1799, Submit Miller, b. Winchendon, July 7, 1777, d. Mch. 1, 1813; m. (2) Jan. 31, 1814, Rachel Holbrook, b. Bellingham, Jan. 17, 1777, d. Oct. 29, 1861. They resided in Westminster. Children: 1. *Cata,*[6] b. Dec. 1, 1799; m. Joel Flagg, b. Grafton, June 7, 1788. They resided in Hubbardston and Westminster. Eleven children. 2. *Dana,* b. Mch. 19, 1801; d. Oct. 24, 1801. 3. *Eda,* b. Aug. 27, 1805; m. Timothy Ellis, b. Franklin, Jan. 1, 1799, son of John and Sarah (Ellis) Jones. They resided in Franklin. She d., and he m. (2) Aug. 16, 1847, Eliza F. Feel of Bellingham. Three children by first wife. 4. *Dorinda,* b. Aug. 27, 1805; d. Aug. 17, 1851; m. Oct. 7, 1829, Almond Coleman of Hubbardston, who d. in Gardner, July 15, 1864. Eight children. 5. *Alfred,* b. Aug. 17, 1807; m. Chloe Blake of East Medway. Four children. 6. *Amos,* b. June 23, 1809; d. April 23, 1883; m. Mch. 27, 1836, Melita Reynolds of Charlton. They resided in Westminster. Four children. 7. *Samantha,* b. Feb. 13, 1811; d. Oct. 16, 1881; m. Dec. 30, 1830, Preston, b. Bellingham, Oct. 28, 1803, son of Timothy and Deborah (Partridge) Ellis, who d. Nov. 19, 1889. Five children. 8. *Dinah Holbrook,* b. Apr. 26, 1815; m. George W. Johnson of Westminster. Three children. 9. *Liberty,* b. May 14, 1817; d. Dec. 21, 1832. 10. *Kendrick,* b. June 22, 1819; d. Aug. 24, 1853; m. Emerency Perham of Royalton. One child.

ii. LEVI, b. Apr. 28, 1777; lived in Charlton; m. and had children.

iii. EDA, b. Feb. 4, 1779; d. Oct. 12, 1832, unmarried.

iv. AMOS, b. Dec. 21, 1781; d. Dec. 30, 1861; m. Nov. 24, 1819, Clarissa (Hill), b. Oct. 18, 1783, in Bellingham, dau. of Aaron and Sally (Coombs) Hill and widow of Asa Slocomb. She d. Jan. 12, 1877. They resided in Bellingham. Children: 1. *Amos,*[6] b. July 15, 1820; d. Feb. 21, 1875, unmarried. 2. *Clarissa,* b. Aug. 5, 1822. 3. *Asa,* b. Dec. 28, 1823; d. Mch. 2, 1865; m. Jan. 4, 1859, Jemima A. Fairbanks, b. Apr. 9, 1829. They resided in Bellingham. Two children. 4. *Charles,* b. Dec. 12, 1827; d. Mch. 23, 1880; m. Nov. 27, 1851, Sophronia M. Graham, b. Nov. 30, 1831. Two children.

v. ELIZABETH, b. Oct. 6, 1783; d. May 29, 1822.

vi. JOSEPH, b. Oct. 13, 1785; d. Aug. 24, 1814; m. Mch. 8, 1812, Lucy, b. Bellingham, Feb. 7, 1784, d. Dec. 3, 1829, dau. of Daniel, Jr., and Charlotte (Legg) Cook. They resided in Bellingham. Children: 1. *Lucy,*[6] b. Dec. 11, 1812; d. June 29, 1837. 2. *Joseph,* b. Mch. 14, 1815; d. Sept. 2, 1866; m. Lydiette Cushman. They resided in Bellingham. Ten children.

vii. BENJAMIN RICHARDSON, b. Sept. 6, 1787; d. Apr. 17, 1873; m. Dec. 18, 1834, Bathsheba, b. Franklin, Apr. 9, 1800, d. May 1, 1882, dau. of John and Sarah (Ellis) Jones. They resided in Bellingham. No children.

viii. SIMON PETER, b. Feb. 5, 1790; d. Oct. 13, 1797.

ix. SIMEON, b. May 17, 1791; d. Oct. 9, 1797.

x. PHILIP, b. Dec. 1, 1792; d. Mch. 10, 1869; m. Dec. 27, 1821, Athina, b. Hopkinton, July 29, 1798, d. Mch. 7, 1879, dau. of Sylvanus and Mary (Smith) Johnson. They resided in Bellingham until 1824, and afterwards, until their deaths, in Franklin. Children: 1. *Catharine Adams,*[5] b. Jan. 18, 1823; m. Apr. 16, 1845, Seth Inman, a widower. Two children. 2. *Susan Johnson*, b. Nov. 7, 1824; m. Oct. 12, 1848, Emerson Newell, b. Mch. 5, 1823, son of Elisha, Jr., and Rena (Fisher) Bullard. Three children. 3. *Irene Richardson*, b. July 18, 1826; d. Mch. 9, 1901; m. Oct. 1, 1851, Asa, b. Petersham, July 7, 1822, son of Partridge and Lucretia (Holbrook) Pond. They resided in Milford. Two sons. 4. *Julia Ann*, b. Dec. 20, 1829; m. Sept. 22, 1852, Aldrich Daniels. Nine children.

xi. DANA, b. Oct. 17, 1794; d. Sept. 30, 1797.
xii. CATA, b. Aug. 5, 1796; d. Oct. 9, 1797.
xiii. ASENETH, b. Feb. 6, 1798; d. Aug. 2, 1841; m. Sept. 13, 1820, Joseph, b. Bellingham, Jan. 23, 1796, d. there Sept. 21, 1870, son of Amos and Abigail (Thayer) Adams. They resided in Bellingham. Four children.

47. ZACHARIAH[4] PARTRIDGE (*Zachariah,*[3] *Eleazer,*[2] *John*[1]) was born in Walpole, Jan. 15, 1744. He settled in Holden, Mass., where he married twice: first, Aug. 31, 1772, Mary Houghton of Holden; and second, Aug. 4, 1779, Mary Whitney of Holden. No records of the births of any children are found.

48. JESSE[4] PARTRIDGE (*Zachariah,*[3] *Eleazer,*[2] *John*[1]) was born in Walpole, Feb. 28, 1748. He married Keziah, born in Walpole, May 12, 1752, died Sept. 1, 1819, daughter of Seth and Mary (Bullard) Clapp. They resided in Walpole for a few years after their marriage, but removed about 1775 to Holden, where they thereafter resided. He was in the Revolutionary service from that town (Mass. Archives). He died in Holden, Mch. 29, 1838, and his will was proved June 20, following. In it he mentions his children, Nancy Hubbard, Lucy Warner, Lewis, Ellis, Jesse and Seth Partridge, and five children of his deceased daughter Charlotte, wife of Asa Smith (Worcester Co. Prob., case 45558). The two oldest children were born in Walpole, the others in Holden.

Children :

i. DAVID,[5] b. Oct. 14, 1771; d. young.
ii. NANCY, b. Dec. 15, 1774; m. Apr. 26, 1804, Samuel Hubbard. Four children.
iii. LUCY, b. May 21, 1776; m. (1) Nov. 7, 1793, Elnathan Davis of Holden, who d. Dec. 30, 1804, aged 43; m. (2) May 1, 1806, Thomas Wilder Warner of Rutland. Six children by first husband; four by second husband.
iv. LEWIS, b. Dec. 2, 1778; d. May 5, 1849; m. Rebecca Maynard; resided in Rutland, Mass., afterwards in Holden, where he d. Children : 1. *Lucy,*[6] b. Jan. 23, 1810. 2. *Lewis*, b. Mch. 11, 1812; d. young.
v. ELLIS, b. Sept. 14, 1781; resided in Holden; m. Joanna ———. Children, b. in Holden: 1. *Charles Billings,*[6] b. May 6, 1808. 2. *Edward Emerson*, b. June 1, 1810; resided in Athol. Two children. 3. *Horace Green*, b. Sept. 26, 1812. 4. *Silas Witt*, b. Dec. 3, 1816; resided in Leicester. Six children. 5. *Julia Ann*, d. in infancy. 6. *Julia Ann*, b. July 9, 1822. 7. *Rufus*.
vi. JESSE, b. Feb. 25, 1784; d. in Princeton, in 1851 or 2; resided in Rutland, Sterling and Princeton; m. Lydia ———. Children, the three oldest b. in Rutland, and burned at Sterling, in a fire which destroyed their father's house: 1. *David,*[6] b. June 1, 1807; d. young. 2. *Moses Maynard*, b. Nov. 26, 1808; d. young. 3. *Warren Clapp*, b. Dec. 3, 1811; d. young. 4. *Roxanna*. 5. *Edward*. 6. *Daniel W.* 7. *Elisha.* 8. *Lyman.* 9. *Emmeline.* 10. *Emmeline.* 11. *Emily.*
vii. SETH CLAPP, b. Jan. 18, 1786.
viii. CHARLOTTE, b. Mch. 30, 1797; m. Mch. 30, 1817, Asa Smith of Leominster. Five children.

49. SAMUEL[4] PARTRIDGE (*Samuel,[3] Samuel,[2] John[1]*) was born in Franklin, Mch. 31, 1741. He married first, Feb. 2, 1764, Keziah, born in Wrentham, Aug. 29, 1735, died May 20, 1771, daughter of Nathaniel and Susanna Hawes. After her death, he appears to have married second, Elizabeth ———. He died Nov. 9, 1776, while in the Revolutionary service. On Apr. 6, 1778, Amos Partridge and the widow Elizabeth were appointed joint administrators of his estate (Suffolk Co. Prob. Rec., vol. lxxii, p. 375). His children, all by his first wife, were born in Wrentham (now Franklin).
   Children:

   i. PHYLETTE,[5] b. Feb. 24, 1765; m. Jan. 22, 1789, in Franklin, Cyrus Kingsbury of Alstead, N. H.
   ii. SYLVESTER, b. Feb. 20, 1766; d. Sept. 5, 1850; m. (1) May 23, 1787, Peggy Morse, who d. Apr. 28, 1790; m. (2) Mch. 10, 1791, Sarah Collins of Franklin, who d. Feb. 4, 1813; m. (3) Feb. 23, 1814, Mrs. Rachel (Brown) Fay, widow of Jesse Fay. She was b. in 1767, and d. May 29, 1861. He resided at Franklin until about 1793, when he removed to Alstead, N. H., where he afterwards lived. Children: 1. *Theron,[6]* b. May 20, 1788; d. Feb. 6, 1858; m. Lydia Rebecca Wentworth, b. at Littleton, Mass., Mch. 23, 1791, d. July 20, 1857, at New Alstead, N. H., where they resided. Three sons. 2. *Peggy,* b. Apr. 27, 1790; d. in 1824. 3. *Samuel,* b. Dec. 19, 1791; d. Oct. 11, 1858; m. in Alstead, N. H., Oct. 25, 1812, Abigail, b. July 1, 1794, d. Oct. 8, 1858, dau. of John and Abigail (Ladd) Ladd. They removed from Alstead, in 1817, to Potsdam, N. Y., where he afterwards lived. Ten children. 4. *Erastus,* b. July 15, 1794; d. Apr. 10. 1812. 5. *Sarah,* b. June 3, 1796; m. Richard Beckwith. Eleven children. 6. *Sylvester,* b. Feb. 7, 1798; d. Aug. 28, 1847; m. May 28, 1827, Judith H., b. Mch. 2, 1803, d. June 29, 1877, dau. of Peter and Deborah Stow, of Newport, N. H. They resided in Evans Mills, Denmark, and Potsdam, N. Y. Seven children. 7. *Lewis,* b. Nov. 17, 1798. 8. *Lydia,* b. Oct. 17, 1802; d. Apr. 10, 1812. 9. *Cyrus,* b. July 13, 1805; d. Apr. 8, 1812. 10. *Alfred,* b. May 3, 1807; d. Apr. 10, 1812. 11. *Lurinda,* b. Oct. 25, 1814; d. Nov. 14, 1888. 12. *Marinda,* b. Oct. 25, 1814; d. Jan. 17, 1889. 13. *Cyrus W.,* b. Sept. 16, 1817; d. May 28, 1881; m. in Potsdam, N. Y., Oct. 21, 1851, Elizabeth Mason. They resided in Potsdam. Two children. 14. *Erastus,* b. Dec. 2, 1820; d. Sept. 26, 1824.
   iii. KEZIAH, b. Nov. 10, 1768; m. Jan. 27, 1793, Samuel Richardson of Alstead, N. H.
   iv. ESTHER, b. May 19, 1776; d. in 1826.

50. AMOS[4] PARTRIDGE (*Samuel,[3] Samuel,[2] John[1]*) was born in Franklin, July 25, 1742. He married, June 17, 1765, Meletiah, born Jan. 31, 1746, in Wrentham, daughter of Joseph and Meletiah (Metcalf) Ellis. He was a lieutenant in the Revolutionary army. He settled in Westford, Vt., after 1788, where he died Aug., 1821. His widow died Mch., 1823. Six of his children were born in Franklin.
   Children:

   i. AMOS,[5] b. Apr. 11, 1777; resided in Westford, Vt., where he d. in 1828. Children: 1. *Addison Bliss,[6]* settled in Fremont, Ill. Two sons. 2. *Samuel,* resided in Westford, Vt. One son. 3. *Amos Dennison,* resided in Appleton, Wis. No children.
   ii. PEARL, b. Jan. 1, 1779.
   iii. APPOLLOS, b. Jan. 18, 1781; d. June, 1827; resided in Westford, Vt. One child: 1. *Albert,[6]* who lived in Westford, and had no children.
   iv. DAVID, b. Aug. 27, 1782; d. unmarried.
   v. ELIZABETH, b. Sept. 21, 1784.

vi. RHODA, b. Jan. 28, 1788.
vii. SAMUEL, resided in Westford, Vt. Children: 1. *Eben,*⁵ settled in Granville, O. Children. 2. *David*, settled in Granville, O. Children. 3. *Ellen C.*, m. —— Bates; resided in Westford. Perhaps Samuel⁵ had other children.

51. REUBEN⁴ PARTRIDGE (*Samuel,*³ *Samuel,*² *John*¹) was born in Franklin, Apr. 14, 1744. He married there, Apr. 7, 1768, Mary Hill. They removed to Keene, N. H., before 1780, and later to Braintree, Vt., where they thereafter resided. They had eight children.

Children:

i. LEWIS,⁵ b. Dec. 15, 1768; d. in infancy.
ii. LEWIS, b. Sept. 7, 1771.
iii. LUCINA, b. July 21, 1773.
iv. LUCRETIA, b. in 1776; d. Aug. 23, 1827; m. Jan. 23, 1793, Ebenezer White of Braintree, Vt., where they resided.
v. DAVID, b. Aug. 15, 1780, in Keene, N. H.; m. May 7, 1806, Polly Riford of Braintree, Vt., where they resided. He d. Jan. 21, 1865. Children: 1. *Sylvander,*⁶ b. Mch. 14, 1807; m. May 20, 1836, Amanda P. Wilcox. One child. 2. *Elmira*, b. Aug. 20, 1808; d. Sept. 10, 1809. 3. *Polly*, b. June 23, 1810; d. Nov. 26, 1881; unmarried. 4. *Vernon David Barron*, b. Apr. 3, 1812; m. Jan. 11, 1843, Lavina R. Platt. 5. *Lucina*, b. May 2, 1814; m. Jan. 24, 1839, Lewis S. Howard. 6. *Louise Elmira*, b. Dec. 2, 1816; m. Aug. 27, 1840, Jeptha Howard, Jr. 7. *Rachel Melinda*, b. Nov. 27, 1818; m. Dec., 1842, Winthrop Sargent. 9. *Joseph*, b. June 23, 1826; d. July 14, 1874; m. Jan. 1, 1854, Lucinda E. Howard.
vi. SAMUEL, b. Jan., 1791; d. July 1, 1859; resided in Braintree, Vt.; m. Mary Bass. Children: 1. *Mary Ann,*⁶ b. Oct. 20, 1821; m. Elisha Mann, Jr. 2. *Edward Martin*, b. June 11, 1824; resided in Pomfret, Vt. 3. *Edwin Orlando*, m. Mary Whitney; went to St. Paul, Minn. 4. *Emmeline*, m. Augustus Harlow.

52. JOSHUA⁴ PARTRIDGE (*Joshua,*³ *Samuel,*² *John*¹) was born in Medway, April 20, 1745. He married, Sept. 24, 1767, Hannah, born Sept. 18, 1744, daughter of John and Hannah (Plimpton) Cutler of Medfield. She died June 19, 1806, in Medway, where they resided. He died Aug. 15, 1802. He was sergeant in Captain Lovell's Co., Fourth Mass. Regiment, in service from Apr. 19, 1775, to Dec. 8, 1776.

Children:

i. JOSEPH,⁵ b. Apr. 26, 1768; d. Oct. 26, 1821; m. Chloe Puffer. Children.
ii. PRISCILLA, b. June 14, 1774; d. Aug. 12, 1774.
iii. DAVID, b. Sept. 20, 1775; d. Apr. 30, 1859; m. Nov. 29, 1804, Miriam, dau. of Samuel Partridge (53). They resided in Brimfield, Mass. Children: 1. *Allen,*⁶ b. Jan. 16, 1806; d. Mch. 8, 1872; m. Dec. 11, 1828, Peggy A. Daniels, b. in Holliston, July 27, 1807, d. June 11, 1887. They resided in Milford, Mass., Harwinton, Conn., and Medway, Mass. Six children. 2. *Mary Ann*, b. Mch. 26, 1808; d. Dec. 27, 1878; m. Apr. 8, 1827, Charles Abbe, b. Feb. 12, 1800, d. July 7, 1877. They resided in Franklin, Mass. Three children. 3. *Warren*, b. at Munson, Mass., Mch. 2, 1810; d. in Boston, Apr. 30, 1871; m. (1) in Sharon, Nov. 20, 1836, Elizabeth, dau. of Jesse and Abigail (Capen) Billings; m. (2) Oct. 26, 1848, Mary Fales Capen, b. Nov. 23, 1815, d. Apr. 14, 1858. They resided in Boston. Four children by first wife.
iv. HANNAH, b. Oct. 3, 1780; d. Sept. 1, 1810, unmarried.
v. SABRA, b. Aug. 5, 1783; d. Nov. 29, 1793.

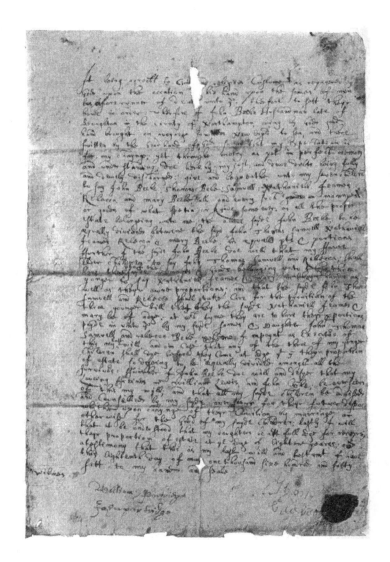

FAC-SIMILE OF WILL OF JOHN BEEBE

53. SAMUEL[4] PARTRIDGE (*Joshua,*[3] *Samuel,*[2] *John*[1]) was born in Medway, Dec. 26, 1752. He married Mehetable, born Mch. 20, 1753, died Jan. 15, 1829, daughter of Elisha and Rebecca (Pratt) Allen. He resided in Medway on the homestead of his father, which, upon his death, he bequeathed to his daughter Mehetabel Daniels. He died Feb. 17, 1842. Some excellent portraits in oil of Samuel and Mehetable Partridge are now in the possession of Mr. William R. Mann of Sharon.

Children :

i. ELIZABETH,[5] b. Apr. 8, 1776; d. Oct. 12, 1861; m. (1) Oct. 15, 1795, Simon Hill; m. (2) Jeremiah Pratt. Four children by first husband; one by second husband.

ii. MATILDA, b. Mch. 9, 1778; d. Nov. 17, 1856; m. (1) Feb. 9, 1797, Oliver Richardson; m. (2) in 1807, Ariah Wheeler. Two children by first husband; one by second husband.

iii. RHODA, b. Dec. 27, 1780; d. Feb. 19, 1869; m. Apr. 19, 1797, Elihu, b. Nov. 29, 1775, d. Mch. 5, 1850, son of Simon and Dinah (Pond) Fisher. Four children.

iv. VESTA, b. Sept. 22, 1782; d. unmarried, in 1800.

v. MIRIAM, b. Aug. 23, 1785; d. Oct. 16, 1842; m. David, son of Joshua Partridge (52).

vi. MEHETABEL, b. Dec. 20, 1788; d. Nov. 7, 1880; m. Mch. 24, 1808, Joseph Daniels. Two sons.

vii. CLARISSA, b. May 17, 1791; d. May 3, 1871; m. Apr. 9, 1818, Fisher Hill. One daughter.

Since this article was compiled, an interesting discovery bearing on the time of departure from England of John and William Partridge (see *ante,* page 3) has been communicated to the author through the courtesy of Mr. L. Bertrand Smith of New York. In Vol. II. of the State Records of Connecticut, on file at the State House in Hartford, may be seen the original will of John Beebe, made on ship-board while on his way to New England. The will, reproduced herewith, bears the date May 18, 1650, and is witnessed by William and John Partridge, whose signatures, it is readily seen by comparing, are identical with those of William and John Partridge of Medfield (see Tilden's Hist. of Medfield, p. 38, and Dedham Records, Town and Selectmen, vol. 3, p. 225).

The name of the ship is not mentioned, nor is it known from what port in England it sailed, or where the passengers landed in America.

The testatator describes himself as "John Beebe, Husbandman, late of Broughton in the County of Northampton."

INDEX OF PERSONS.